The Definitive Spa and Body Therapist's Handbook

The 5 Keys to unlimited energy, balance and bliss

First published by O Books, 2008
O Books is an imprint of John Hunt Publishing
Ltd., The Bothy, Deershot Lodge, Park Lane,
Ropley, Hants, SO24 0BE, UK
office1@o-books.net
www.o-books.net

Distribution in:

UK and Europe
Orca Book Services
orders@orcabookservices.co.uk
Tel: 01202 665432 Fax: 01202 666219 Int. code
(44)

USA and Canada
NBN
custserv@nbnbooks.com
Tel: 1 800 462 6420 Fax: 1 800 338 4550

Australia and New Zealand
Brumby Books
sales@brumbybooks.com.au
Tel: 61 3 9761 5535 Fax: 61 3 9761 7095

Far East (offices in Singapore, Thailand, Hong
Kong, Taiwan)
Pansing Distribution Pte Ltd
kemal@pansing.com
Tel: 65 6319 9939 Fax: 65 6462 5761

South Africa
Alternative Books
altbook@peterhyde.co.za
Tel: 021 555 4027 Fax: 021 447 1430

Text copyright Tara J Herron 2008

Design: Stuart Davies

ISBN: 978 1 84694 097 2

Printed by Chris Fowler International
www.chrisfowler.com

O Books operates a distinctive and ethical publishing philosophy in
all areas of its business, from its global network of authors to
production and worldwide distribution.
This book is produced on FSC certified stock, within ISO14001
standards. The printer plants sufficient trees each year through
the Woodland Trust to absorb the level of emitted carbon in
its production.

The Definitive Spa and Body Therapist's Handbook

The 5 Keys to unlimited energy, balance and bliss

Tara J Herron

BOOKS

Winchester, UK
Washington, USA

CONTENTS

Chapter Four

Dedication

In gratitude for my body that breathes, sees, hears, feels, thinks
and lives to share in the beauty of the elements we call earth and
to all beings everywhere.
May this handbook be a friend to many.

PROLOGUE

PRIMAL SPA

*T*he promenade of small squat juniper trees lead me down the dusty hillside where I have been communing all afternoon with the sweet smell of sun-drenched alfalfa grass high up on the hills of Harbin Hot Springs. This is the ceremonial ground where our tribal Indian ancestors led their sacred medicine circles. My brown skin is wrapped in a simple white sarong, pulled comfortably through my legs and round my waist like a loin cloth. My breasts are free to merge with the intensely clean hot air. Black hair laps down my back cooling me, warding off the flies as my sandaled feet roll over the loose dry stones. My mind is a warm pasture of pleasured peace. The path changes into flatter land and the heady scent of fresh figs draws my hands up to the large black succulents that hang provocatively above me. One, two, three, maybe four I absorb into the well of my body relishing the vibrancy of their historic life. Passing over the little broken arched bridge the stream sings to me, reminding me that soon it will be dark. I tread carefully stepping over a coiled snake asleep on the woodland path and find that I am chanting `om mahne padme hum` over and over again.*

The strong pungency of sulphur comes wafting in as the sound of heavy running water reaches my ears. The baths await me in their simple temple of stone and antiquity. The worn wood decks are dotted with a few others sitting alone or in groups, their naked skin as much a part of this holy landscape as the old bay trees that shelter us. I wash off the dust and enter the sanctuary of the steaming hot mineral pool as it pours cease-lessly from deep beneath the earth's surface. It is twilight, my favourite time, when the veil between the worlds seems to open invitingly. Someone has placed fresh flowers above the mouth of the spring and candles flicker in the fading light. The small enclosure holds the energy of the space in a natural peace where no-one speaks in words, just smiles and sighs. I move slowly onto the first step down into the water and pause to breathe, the heat penetrates with an intensity that takes courage to receive. At each new step down I pause and allow my body to adjust to the seething temperature that seeks out the resistance, enticing me to accept and let go. Inch by inch I edge into this magical cauldron that melts every atom of resistance, of interference from my body and mind. I am standing up to my neck, leaning against the worn soft stone wall immersed in the power of these healing waters that quenches every part of me. I am liquid fire, burning like molten rock, dissolving the dross. After a while I wade the short distance to where the water flows in and place my head beneath its abundant baptism.

Reborn, like the phoenix, I rise up out of the fire waters and lie flat on my back on the old oak bench to cool. My skin dries instantly and I am so relaxed, purified, weightless, boundless and blissful, luxuriating in this Garden of Eden. After a while I move toward the cold pool sheltered amidst a labyrinth of trees where I submerge and re-balance my whole being. Sensational fireworks explode through me as my pores close and blood rushes to my head.

On the deck the yoga practice is beginning as the dusk holds court in the crystal clear mountain air. The emerging postures pay homage to the sanctuary of this timeless territory and we equally breathe the living and de-composing molecules of life with unreserved acceptance. My heart sculptures the syllables of this heavenly moment, resonating in feelings of gratitude and thankfulness. The body prayers move to our throat and lips which chant the symbols of a vibrational language that bridges country and culture and sound the universal words of the soul.

PREFACE

We are drawn to the spa for sanctuary and renewal, within an environment that has become the antithesis of our fast paced, high-tech world, where we retreat into the vital elements of life. The focus on 'healing environments' has emphasised the quality of touch, smell, hearing, seeing and sensing to bring us into harmony with a natural state of being where we are no longer required 'to do', rather 'to be.'

A world-wide fusion of influences has united the spirit of the spa, into a place where we go to reconnect with our inner selves, our soul, and experience that joyous sense of gratitude for simply being alive that comes so easily when you feel good! This journey through the elements nurtures the body yet takes us beyond its finite form into a timelessness and serenity where we are content to simply breathe, happy in our own skin.

The spa has become the new monastery, the house of the spirit, a place where we all become one in the anonymity of robes, shared baths, bareness, peace and the mutual respect we hold for each others space. The mystical quality of human consciousness is reflected in these temples of repose, where the hands-on therapist creates the bridge across the divide from chaos to peace, from stress to balance, guiding us further on to touch base with our inner gods, whoever they may be, bringing us home to ourselves.

Within this spa renaissance, that draws much of its knowledge from ancient cultures, the variations of facilities linking themselves to the gender of spa-ing range from urban day spas to cruise ship extravaganzas and many other variations defined later in Your

Space. The authentic and not so authentic – yet all serve a purpose. To create an alternate reality of primal stimulation that allows us to let go of the restrictions imposed by day- to- day life, to feel free and relaxed, beautiful and balanced, from the inside out. Within these elemental sanctuaries we can dissolve into a renewed sense of being that reforms us, generating an easy living response.

With the rise in popularity of de-stressing and relaxing treatments massage is statistically the number one treatment requested throughout the world. The growth in spa culture is unprecedented and a recent survey* shows it has increased by 129% since 2002 across all continents. Today people from all walks of life flock to these kinetic sanctuaries in droves hoping to escape the hard edged reality of daily life. For spa goers this is almost sacred time when an ultimate peace is sought to transform our inner selves and attain, perhaps, a sense of perfection.

The spa environment is essentially rooted in the harmonious orchestration of natural elements that awaken our senses, allowing our bodies to let go of resistance; of strife on every level. Journeying through the rituals of the spa provide us with the opportunity to be touched energetically by these elements, infusing a connection with the natural world. Our pursuit for wellbeing has become a lifestyle priority making the spa an ultimate destination.

Evolving Beauty
The welcome shift in our perception of what amounts to 'being beautiful' continues to evolve as our awareness grows. The integration of more ethnic beauty regimes from different cultures has introduced all of us to a more universal account of what equates to beauty and how we quantify it. With people being born from parents whose origins may come from opposite sides of the globe we now see extraordinary and exotic human beings with perhaps a mix of Turkish and Scandinavian or African and Indian that break through the conceptual moorings of traditional looks, and skin types. Ancient principles of skin care are rising to the fore once again, as Ayurvedic wisdom from India or Mayan beauty

rituals from South America are studied and brought into a universal spa experience.

Being seen as beautiful, now stems from a deeper understanding of how being healthy and happy are visible factors in the overall vision of how we appear to others, as well as to ourselves. As our inner perceptions change so does our outer vision. The realization that beauty is more than skin deep has now developed into an active pursuit of generating an inner harmony that is free from stress, tension and toxicity. Yoga, aromatherapy, de-tox treatments, meditation, nutrition, reiki healing, plus many massage based therapies have all risen to the forefront of leading a healthy lifestyle and are often integrated into the philosophy and practice of a beauty treatment.

The growing cultivation of holistic beauty treatments are now actual rituals, that embrace the principles of our psycho-physiology, the relationship between our mind and body, to reveal a deeper sense of beauty that comes from within, shining out from an inner peace of mind and a deeply relaxed, comfortable body. The results from this approach prove to be superior in more ways than a superficial skin care standard. Holistic beauty treatments that include massage techniques and elements of relaxation help to dissolve physical tensions and psychological stress that contribute towards breaking up tense holding patterns and cell regeneration, thereby slowing down the aging process.

An experience of inner peace and serenity resolves issues of psychological conflict with the inevitable changes that occur through hormonal elements, creating a sense of 'growing old gracefully'. Qualities of inner peace create space to let go of the past and embrace the present with renewed understanding and poise. A holistic approach can connect to the heart of the client, also relieving emotional anxiety and therefore uplifting the spirit.

Traditional beauty therapists or technicians in the spa environment are now involved in this more holistic way of working, yet are often not given enough training or awareness of the philosophy behind the shift in our evolving perception of beauty. The spa environment offers the perfect balance of elements to create this sense of well-being and a natural feeling of beauty.

This book is offered also to these therapists as a way of enriching and supporting you as an individual, and in your skills.

The Evolving Therapist

Where there is need there is demand and for the management this thirst for 'renewal' means more conscious, intelligent and sensitive resources are required to fulfil this surge of energy, this pilgrimage to the spa. To find ways of creating a renewable support structure for your team of therapists, so that they too feel cared for in the spirit of the spa. The therapist is at the heart of the spa experience and care of their well-being is fundamental to the successful results you aim for on all levels. An imbalanced, stressed and unhappy therapist equals a disturbed client! The aim of this book is to give you the knowledge and techniques to help support the heart of your service.

For the hands- on therapist a busy spa can mean long working days where they may carry out consecutive massage- related sessions for up to 8 hours with only short breaks. The impact on their physical, mental and emotional well -being can create extreme imbalance which ultimately can affect the quality of the total spa experience. Massage therapy is one of *the* most demanding physical therapies that both holistic and beauty practitioners carry out on a daily basis. And it is historically one of the most effective and enjoyable ways of de-stressing body and mind.

The role of the therapist often goes beyond the expectation of the prescribed therapy, beyond the boundaries of your everyday mind, into the deeper subconscious needs of the client without therapist or client realizing it. These unconscious and unspoken needs can draw on the therapists` essential inner resources affecting your body, your subconscious mind and general well being.

As a result many massage- based therapists and holistic health practitioners feel completely drained at the end of a day, or even after working with one particular client and wonder why. Physical exhaustion, aches and pains; unreasonable negativity or experiences of psychological stress, and emotional tension can draw on the therapist's vital energy.

You want to know why this is happening and seek a deeper understanding and practical ways of protecting your self to maintain optimum balance.

Healer – Heal Thyself. These prophetic words spoken by Hippocrates, the founder of the concept of modern medicine and healing, is more pertinent now than ever.

You may ask yourself, What does it mean to "give healing"'? How do I feel more at peace within myself? How can I prevent feeling drained after giving a session? Why does my lower back hurt? Why do my hands ache? How can I prevent these feelings? Why do I feel dizzy? How do I support myself in the process of supporting the needs of my client? Is it right to massage hour after hour with no break? How do I keep on top of it all?"

And there may be other purely practical questions bothering you. "What is the difference between a hotel spa or destination spa? How do I make myself more employable? Which skills are most in demand? Are my working conditions at their best for both client and therapist? Do I need more training? Am I safe and do I have full legal protection? How should I handle things if I believe a certain client risks acting inappropriately?

These questions are some of the motivating elements driving The Spa Therapists Handbook giving you the keys to empower and protect your self and your space in preparation for and during your work. This guidebook will give you the understanding, facts and techniques to help you find inner and outer balance, insight and strength to support you and your clients.

Therapist as Heart of the Spa

Having myself lived and trained since 1980 in the pure air of natural hot mineral spas and meditation retreats, as well as luxury hotel spas and retreats in America, Asia and the UK, plus experienced treatments from the sublime to the ridiculous, I write this book from the fabric of my being that is well steeped in the ancient and modern traditions and trends of spa culture. I have worked in all aspects of the spa industry from therapist to trainer, employed and self-employed, consultant and manager; product development to branding and bespoke treatment design to simple lover of a really superb massage and spa experience. Wherever I go as a guest or a trainer I am aware of the same issues and asked the same questions over and over again. Therefore I bring this knowledge to you as an accessible offering to all spa therapists.

Exceed your own expectations and invite the miraculous into your life. Invest in yourself, give time to feel and sense who you really are and who you can become. Keep training, keep learning, keep developing your skills and enriching your inner being which is at the very heart of all that you share as a therapist in a healing profession. Allow yourself to be inspired by opening your mind and heart to new ideas, concepts and experiences. The journey along a skilful path is also a journey into rediscovering your full potential. Dream in colour and live in colour. You are your own best client and you are at the very heart of the spa journey.

Therefore, training is also at the heart of the spa industry and how you care for yourself as a soulful therapist is paramount in the success from every angle we care to observe.

This book highlights the Five Keys that together paint the holistic picture of a balanced way of working and being that reaches into the heart of what you need and want to know.

INTRODUCTION

The Five Keys
to Unlimited Energy & Therapeutic Balance

The following five keys are designed to cultivate the growing awareness of your inner being, offering clarity and guidance of the influential areas that enhance your skills.

Your Body Your posture and body awareness is fundamental to supporting your vehicle for practicing demanding physical therapies.

Your Breathing If you are not breathing fully, your client is not breathing! Your breath is at the very centre of how your energy circulates and releases. A tool that supports, transforms and relaxes.

Your Mind The quality of your thoughts, consciousness and intention are at the pivot of how you relate to and transform your creative work experience.

Your Spirit Your alignment with the resource of Universal Energy is directly connected to your insight, sensitivity and healing potential that protects and guides you through spiritual principles.

Your Space Understand the definition, purpose and benefits of each spa space.

Be clear on your employment, contracts and training opportunities. How you prepare, cleanse and relate to the space in which you work is an essential element to maintain balance, energy, safety and enjoyment.

Intelligent Wisdom

The Five Keys together comprise the wholeness of your experience as a therapist which puts the **wisdom** back together with your intelligence, skill, and environment. This is for the Whole Therapist.

This handbook draws on the Ayurvedic analogue of `wholeness` as the cornerstone philosophy for understanding the inter-relationship of all the elements needed to operate wholeheartedly as a spa therapist. It is one thing to have an intelligent grasp of therapeutic techniques on practical or theoretical levels, but is that really enough? In today's world people come for spa therapy because they want to feel really good, deep down inside, not just for superficial reasons or to treat one particular symptom. Therapists need and want to know how to respond to this universal factor in such a way that you utilise all aspects of your body, mind and soul so that you include and balance yourself in the process of treating others.

Ayurveda, which means `the science of life`, explains its fundamental philosophy of 'wholeness' by describing what happens when only the highly potent medicinal element of a plant is extracted, leaving behind the plant itself. This is understood as extracting the `**intelligence**` of the plant but leaving behind the `**wisdom.**`. Taking the medicine but not the healing! This means that the essence is aborted from its natural environment and therefore looses touch with its original source of energy, life and spirit - the plants` **consciousness**! And as like attracts like, the way the plants` potential power works will be diminished by not being its 'whole plant self,' and therefore not *wholly digested* thoroughly by the receiver.

The Story of Two

What really goes on in the treatment room varies dramatically from one therapist to another; from place to place; from country to country. Influences generated by culture, climate, country or hotel spa, city salon, cruise spas or private settings all have *some i*mpact on how therapists are able to fulfil their role. Yet the immediate dynamic of therapist to client roughly remains the same.

We must also consider that the clients` expectations will differ based on their past experiences, the spa location, the products, the treatment cost and the brochure description, as well as the skill, empathy and inner nature of the therapist. These are the common elements that influence a hands-on experience generating the vast differences from one treatment to the next. However, there are some basic fundamental facts that are common to all situations.

Primarily there are usually two people in the treatment room; two people in touch with each other and breathing together. Two people listening together and experiencing each other. The physical proximity of body work, massage or beauty treatment could *not* be much closer. This proximity generates a certain chemistry, a special relationship where an alchemy, the potential for change and transformation, is organically taking place.

The client may never have met you before yet they are entrusting you with their naked body, with all its beauty and imperfections, lying on the couch for you to touch them. This simple manoeuvre carries with it the threads to an ancient history of massage rituals and use of oils to anoint and heal, as far back as the Ancient Egyptian and Mayan cultures and probably before that. Massage- based treatments also resembles very primal experiences we have as human beings from being babies swaddled in towels by our parents and carers, to being nursed or healed when ill, to the preamble of a more sexual intimacy. All these shrouds and memories can be brought to the couch in the hidden recesses of the clients psyche and genetic inheritance as human beings.

During hands- on therapy the recipient may experience a range of emotion from irritability to mild enjoyment and indifference, to far more intense feelings of joy, sadness, release, love and even bliss. Sometimes people may involuntarily cry, laugh or see colours and visions of distinct character. The experience can be so deeply relaxing that clients sleep, dream, twitch and sigh as their body, mind and emotions unravel and let go.

Within this complex internal environment where sessions can last more than an hour, the client may process a great deal of personal issues which the therapist may unknowingly absorb and not understand how to process within themselves!

Giving and Receiving

The natural dynamic of *giving* body therapy automatically puts the therapist in the role of 'Giver' or Facilitator and the client becomes the 'Taker' or Receiver. The situation is a two- way street where both people are in direct connection with each other, inevitably reflecting and affecting one another.

You may have noticed how as a therapist you can come out of a session thinking it was the best treatment you ever gave, feeling re-energised and inspired. On a simple level, an open, positive client can equally bring out the best in you, as a negative client can bring out the worst. This is because the positive client is free of blockages and unconscious resistance which allows *you to give more easily*. The client is truly *receiving* you and therefore naturally giving back that which is being given. This automatically allows your energy to flow more freely, regenerating itself as your life-force is holistically re-cycled.

However, this is not always the case. Where the client is burdened by resistance, criticism or neediness, or perhaps carrying the destructive nature of negative thoughts (which may well be unconscious) the therapist`s energy will not be fully received; will *not be taken*. It will be like knocking on a door that just won`t open! This dynamic blocks the flow of energy *through* the therapist *to the* client, who finds it hard to receive and let go. Here the therapist needs to use techniques that encourage the client to trust and release whilst circulating any build up within yourself, otherwise you will be exhausted by their resistance.

And following suit, if your ability to *give* is limited by your own tensions, distractions or blind spots, your energy will quickly run dry causing similar symptoms of stress and imbalance.

In light of the demand placed on therapists it is essential that you receive the knowledge and support you require. This Handbook will give you the core principles of hands on therapy to help guide you through your working day and add another dimension to your lifes' journey.

Growing Spa Awareness

In addition to these universal factors people who frequent spas and enjoy treatments are often well- seasoned spa goers and travellers who have a breadth of experience in massage therapies. These are discerning consumers who may even know more than you do about the techniques and levels of excellence that can be practiced. Now people from all walks of life take courses and learn how to do a variety of therapies, if only to use on their friends and family. Therefore they will have quite an in-depth working knowledge and higher level of expectation. The world is certainly a smaller place and with the growth of spas and merging cultures, plus the increase in popularity of massage therapy, the general level of expertise needs to be raised.

As many therapists now work for luxury salons and spas you are not in control of the appointment book or what prices people pay for treatments. Therefore, even though you may not feel you can give four or five £100 treatments in a row you are expected to perform almost to the minute!

Most of these establishments use product brands that do provide training which enables therapists to carry out the required treatment menu to a functional level of performance. However, as some therapists may have only recently qualified from colleges in basic massage skills on a predominantly beauty- based course, these training courses often do not give enough time to learn or practice new techniques to a genuinely competent level.

Every therapist is different and some require more information and practice than others to perfect their skills and mature within themselves. When possible, individual coaching goes a long way in gaining valuable personal experience leading to a more tangible self-confidence that benefits the client, spa team and therapist alike.

The immediate work environment may also be a challenging, demanding and busy place that requires the therapist to clean, orchestrate laundry, sell products and even use highly advanced

IT on reception. Yet, when you know how to create your own inner and outer balance, being clear on what is expected from you by your employers and colleagues, you can work harmoniously to your full potential.

The more you can help yourself
the more you are able to positively help your clients
Your ability to help someone else is primarily based in your own self awareness and inner balance. First you need to know how to help yourself as a starting point for mastering the skills needed to help another.

Self Knowledge leads to Self Mastery and will protect you from unnecessary stress, injury and confusion.

Remember, it is you the therapist, your wisdom, power and skill, who sets the tone of the treatment and so it is in your interests to help yourself in as many ways as possible. Self awareness can give you 'boundaries', a 'sense of self', that will naturally prepare you for any eventuality and protect you from occupational stress. Developing clear and intelligent boundaries help you to know how *you* really feel and recognise what belongs to you and what belongs` to the other person. You can then 'hold your space', thereby saving vital energy to support your work as a therapist.

CHAPTER ONE

KEY NUMBER ONE

YOUR BODY

Your mind is the map, your body is the territory

T Herron

Your body is your vehicle; it is your major tool and prized equipment that requires maintenance and fine tuning to be able to run the marathon of long body work sessions time after time. Your body is a complex network of subtle and dense physical components that are constantly being employed to perform specific movements.

Practicing body-work therapy is like a sport that demands balanced, well trained techniques to sustain your focus, stamina and effectiveness. Therefore, it is vital to counter balance the effects of negative stress on the body with techniques that help you maintain physical balance, flexibility and core strength. These techniques will help you build your store house of resources, tap into universal energy, prevent weakness and repetitive strain injury. And, keep you grounded.

Body therapy can also be compared to playing a musical instrument where we have to know the instrument well to be able to 'tune it up'and play it harmoniously. This also applies to how you use your own body as the key instrument in creating an effective treatment. And, like all instruments that are played repeatedly, your body can easily become out of tune and worn down, feeling out of touch with your inner harmony, attunement and core centre. First we have to understand the signs of disharmony in the physical aspects of our body to be able to correct it; to know where it is out of tune; not only having a firm grasp of the anatomy, but also of the more subtle elements of balance.

Often blind people make powerful therapists due to their sense of touch and feeling being far more developed as they do not rely on the eye to automatically guide them.

Like brail, massage and body therapies reveal the meaning of what is written through feeling the shape and texture of the formation beneath your hands. Try closing your eyes sometimes during a massage and you will feel how you begin to see with your fingers and develop a greater sensitivity to what is going on beneath the surface of the clients' skin and your own sensory awareness. You will also become more attuned to your inner balance and posture which is intensified when your eyes are closed and you cannot see three- dimensionally.

So your first priority is to tune up your own body, take care and nurture your well being and vital energy as an important part of the equation of the client-therapist dynamic.

Potential effects of giving body work

Positively	Negatively
Tones muscles	Lower lumbar back pain
Mobilizes the joints	Sciatica
Improves circulation	Tightness across the shoulders
Softens the hands	Stiff and unyielding neck
Cardio vascular benefits the heart	Dizziness
Feeling grounded	Shortness of breath
Calming	Weakness in the wrists
Centring	Aching fingers
Spiritually uplifting	Carpal tunnel syndrome
Matures insight	Erases boundaries

Develops boundaries
Cultivates compassion
Self healing
Balances breathing

Head-aches
Cramping in legs
Digestive problems
Develops sensitivity
Exhaustion
Irritability
Allergies
De-hydration

Balance through your Posture

Your spine is the rod, the central trunk that supports your posture keeping your back upright and balanced. Maintaining a flexible yet strong spine, like a young tree that bends in the wind is a vital part of your physical well-being. As the saying goes 'young trees bend in the wind, old trees fall. ' This is also referring to the sap, the fluids that flow freely through your body which are replenished through de-toxification, exercise and rehydration. Dehydration is one of the main causes of energy blockages in the body. The roots of poor posture stem from your spinal alignment and if an imbalance is held for long, will automatically weaken the muscles and put undue pressure on your joints.

When the vertebrae are imbalanced this in turn puts pressure on the central nervous system and the corresponding sympathetic nerves, which channel energy to all your internal body parts. This pressure can reduce the amount of energy flowing to those important organs and limbs, especially the ones you need for work which include your heart, lungs, abdomen, hips, legs, feet, shoulders, arms, neck, head and hands.

Maintaining a healthy spinal alignment as you work around the massage couch influences many systems of your body network.

Height of your couch

The simple fact of the height of your therapy couch may be one of the causes of your low energy or back pain. The correct couch height will in itself help to support your posture and ability to massage effectively. When a traditional couch is required for treatments, stooping over a couch that is too low or the raised tense shoulders of a couch that is too high for you, can restrict your energy, strain muscles and cause persistent back-pain leading to further complications.

As a rule the height of the couch should be measured from the level of your knuckles when you are standing upright with your arms by your sides. Though different types of body-work demand

varying angles and manoeuvres that may require the couch height to be lower or higher. New therapeutic techniques are being introduced all the time so make sure you know which is the best couch height for *your height*, and the treatment requirement.

Most spas today have electrically operated couches where it is quick and easy to adjust, as well as other body support features that are ergonomically designed to give your client a more body-friendly and comfortable treatment. And help you in the

Measure couch to knuckles for optimum height.

process. However, where couches have to be manually adjusted, it is obviously better to have a dedicated room for each therapist so that the set-up is suited to the individual.

Balancing your Seat

Likewise, if you need or prefer to sit for body- work sessions, which may be a facial, reflexology or cranial therapy, make sure the height of your chair also supports your techniques. Innovativce ergonomically designed stools that rock slightly back and forth, allowing your lower back more movement are now available. They increase the flow of energy up and down your spine, through to your shoulders and into your hands. This is far superior to static chairs or stools that fix your spinal position poorly and for too long, limiting the circulation of your 'chi' vital energy.

Many people these days are using gym-balls for seated therapy which also adds another therapeutic dimension to the treatment room and this energises the connection between therapist and client. This way of working can also be used in spa reception areas where receptionists are tied to a desk, perhaps for hours. Gym balls help to keep the spinal energy mobile and therefore the body and mind are more refreshed.

Gym balls are not suitable for all treatments.

Are you short circuiting?
The following posturing techniques prolong your physical energy and stamina, preventing lower back pain and injury, improving your fitness, ease and effectiveness.

Short Circuiting is a term used when you only use your upper body strength and energy, ie: your arms, shoulders and hands to carry out massage techniques. Doing so will burn out your energy in no time and can cause serious physical imbalance. This is also true even if you work with your elbows or forearms as well as your hands for deeper techniques. Short circuiting utilises a very small cycle of energy that cannot sustain itself over such prolonged use and eventually there can be damage to your muscle tissue, vertebrae and joints. This also reduces the circulation and therefore oxygen to the brain and to the lower part of your body.

Short circuiting your energy taxes the heart, puts unnecessary stress on your neck and may be the cause of headaches and dizziness. This happens because you are only using superficial 'finite' muscle strength rather than the dynamic 'infinite' re-vitalising energy that is available to you as it comes *into* your lower body from the earth beneath you.

When your stance and posture are balanced you will find unlimited power and energy to effectively massage for longer. Your arms and hands can then draw on a more 'renewable' source of strength and be freed up to attune themselves to the more sensitive issues of massage therapy.

Working in this way also protects you from the potential hazards of repetitive strain injury and exhaustion.

Working from your lower body

When you are working around the couch always make sure that your legs are at least 2 ft apart. If your feet are too close together you reduce the amount of energy circulating between your legs imbalancing your hips. When the legs are too close together the body tends to bend from the lower back muscles, eventually causing excessive strain to the lower lumbar region of your spine. This potentially creates chronic back pain, sciatica and possibly a slipped vertebral disc.

Creating a space between your feet your upper body mobility will naturally be enhanced. You will be able to reach further with your hands without putting undue stress on your lower back, shoulders, scapulae or arms. This is because you will be using your *hips and legs* to guide your upper body, instead of your lower back. Your hips will have a wider range of movement supported by the flexibility in your knees *to bend* in the direction of your hips when your legs are apart.

By working in this way you are utilising the power and strength of your thighs to draw more energy through your hips and up your body to your arms and hands. You will easily experience how effortless and correct this way of working feels.

When the legs are together this tends to weaken your 'centre of gravity', located at the navel and directly linked with the roots at the base of your spine. The base of your spine is the *negative pole*, the grounding force, which implies it is the 'receiving' end of your spinal column that connects with the resourceful energy from the earth as it travels up your spine empowering your body. When your legs are apart the access to this energy will be greatly improved as the *base line* is broader and more open. All marshal arts and tai-chi work along this same principle of balance.

Try this basic exercise to prevent back strain and increase your energy

Core Strength – Center of Gravity Stretch One
Stand with your legs about 2 feet apart.

Turn your feet outwards.

Lift your arms out in front of you to the level you would need to give massage.

Turn your hips to the left.

Notice your upper body and arms also moving to the left.

Bend your left knee and reach with your arms further towards the left.

Then bring the arms back to centre, straightening your left knee.

Now turn your hips to the right.

Notice your upper body and arms also moving to the right.

Bend your right knee and reach with your arms further to the right.

Then bring the arms back to centre, straightening your right knee.

Relax your arms down.

Repeat this exercise 3 times on either side and notice how your range of movement extends and also reduces the strain on your lower lumbar, back muscles.

Core Strength Centre of Gravity Stretch Two

**Now try the same exercise with your breath for maximum
energy and safety**
Stand with your legs about 2 feet apart.
Turn your feet outwards.
Breathe in and lift your arms out in front of you to your couch
level.
Breathe out and turn your hips to the left.
Breathing in notice your upper body and arms also moving to the
left. *Breathe out* and bend your left knee, reaching out with your
arms further towards the left.
Breathe in and bring your arms back to centre, straightening your
left knee and *Breathe out* at the centre.
Breathe in and turn your hips to the right, noticing your arms also
moving to the right.
Breathe out and bend your right knee and reach out with your
arms further to the right.
Breathe in and bring your arms back to centre, straightening your
right knee.
Breathing in relax your arms down.

Again, repeat this exercise 3 times on either side to help you
become familiar with the posture. We will discuss more about
breathing in the chapter Your Breath.

Aching hands and wrists
Your hands need healing and restoring on a regular basis to help
them maintain flexibility and ease as you work. Many therapists
complain of aching joints in the fingers and wrists which is an
occupational hazard of repeating the same movements daily
without re-balancing them.

Hand Soak Revival
**This is a wonderful practice at the end of a long day, to not
only reduce pain and tension but also release toxins and lactic**

acids.

Fill a bowl with hot water.

Place relaxing or purifying salts in the water till they dissolve

You can also add essential oils to help aches and pains such as black pepper, ginger, lavender, chamomile and frankincense.

Sit down comfortably and soak your hands for at least 15 – 20 minutes.

Afterwards massage therapeutic oils or creams into them.

Finger and Wrist Stretch Exercise One

Place palms against each other with fingers and thumbs stretched wide apart.

Lift the palms away from each other whilst pressing the finger of each hand against each other.

Flex the palms up and down to stretch the fingers.

Finger and Wrist Stretch Exercise Two

Interlock your fingers.

Turn your palms away from you stretching the fingers back.

Stretch out your arms in front of you and hold.

Now lift your arms and inter-locked hands above your head.

Stretch up and hold.

Wrist Release One

Rotate hands from the wrists in both directions. At least 6 times

Wrist, Hand and Shoulder Release Two

Interlock the fingers behind your back with palms upward.

Bend forward slowly from the waist.

Bring your arms up behind you stretching the shoulders back as much as you can.

Hold and pull up with the hands to stretch the wrists.

After 60 seconds release your hands down to the floor.

Let yourself hang down and relax.

Whole Hand Revival

Standing with your legs apart bring your hands up to chest level.

Begin to shake your hands up and down as if you were flicking off water.

Let your hands move up and down faster and faster.

Just let them become really loose and floppy as you shake them like a bunch of bananas.

After a minute or so just let them pause out in front of you and feel the energy and magnetism in your hands.

Relax them.

Finger Joint Release

Grip each finger one- by- one and rotate in both directions.

Then pull the finger outwards just to the level that is comfortable to you.

Carpal Tunnel Syndrome

Carpal Tunnel Syndrome is a painful condition of the wrist, thumb and index finger which is caused by inflammation of the tissue putting pressure on the median nerve from the wrist to the hand. The root causes stem from over use of the fingers, hand and wrist creating a repetitive strain injury, but also can be linked to diabetes, rheumatoid arthritis or glandular imbalance in the pituitary or thyroid. Consequently it is vital to get the symptoms professionally diagnosed by a doctor, osteopath or chiropractor.

Symptoms range from tingling and pain, to numbness, hyper sensitivity and weakness in the hand and wrist. In most situations particularly when treated early on, the condition can be healed successfully to complete recovery.

Ways to treat CTS
Once the condition has been identified there a few courses of action you can take:

Rest your hand and do not use for up to 3 weeks and see if condition improves.

Stretching exercises for your thumb, fingers and wrists. Yoga stretches are one of the most effective ways of relieving and treating the condition.

Acupuncture can help relieve pain and symptoms.

Sleep with your arm supported by a pillow so that it is at a slight angle.

Deep Massage with oils improves circulation and to reduces inflammation.

Wearing a splint at night to accelerate the healing process.

Wearing a wrist support during the day to protect and improve strength.

Surgery is very common for CTS where no other treatment has worked BUT this is a very last resort and can be healed with the above.

Ways to prevent CTS
Hands-free massage techniques
Learn massage techniques where you use your forearms and elbows to balance out the stress on your hands. These techniques

are very helpful for working on the back and shoulders which can be extremely demanding on your fingers and wrists.

Courses in Hands-Free massage techniques are more available now as the need for this approach is a priority for the busy therapist. Also, receive regular hand and arm massage and practice yoga at least once a week.

Practice the exercises recommended for hands on a regular basis.

Scoliosis of the spine

Scoliosis of the spine is a condition that can be developed in childhood where a distinct curvature of the spinal vertebrae becomes part of your skeletal holding pattern. This condition can cause further stress on the back support muscles and central nervous system. These symptoms can not only be painful but in turn may lower energy levels considerably due to pressure on the sympathetic nervous system that is responsible for channelling energy to all the vital organs. Long hours of standing or sitting around a couch with your arms and neck in a certain posture can further irritate a curvature of the spine.

If you suffer from this or think you might it is definitely worth going for periodic visits to a cranial osteopath or cranio-sacral therapist or chiropractor that has been recommended to you. There are some excellent ones and well.. some not so excellent! In addition to this you need to join a Hatha or Iyengar yoga class that focuses on postures in a gentle way to help you stretch, align and redress the balance. The suggested poses presented later on in this chapter will give you a worthwhile routine to practice.

Keep in mind that your body is the key instrument of your work so maintaining a happy and stress-free physical state is your priority. If you carry an excessive amount of tension whilst you work your level of connection with your client will be greatly reduced. In addition, the blockages in your body will create potential areas of further congestion as energy will not be able to flow freely through you.

Helpful exercise for scoliosis
At the end of long sessions practice this re-balancing stretch.
Stand straight with your arms extended above your head.
Make sure the palms of your hands are facing each other.
Inhale and stretch up.
Exhale and bend slowly to the right.
Inhale and return to the centre.
Exhale and bend slowly to the left.
Inhale and return to the centre.
Repeat this SLOWLY twice on each side and then breathe with hands in central position above your head.
Just let your arms float slowly down to your sides.

Sciatica

The sciatic nerve is the largest and longest nerve in the body running down from the sacral region of the lower back along the back of your legs to the ankles and feet. Imbalance in the sacroiliac joint or poor posture in general can put pressure on this sensitive nerve resulting in pain ranging from a deep throbbing ache to intense sharp waves. If you have left this condition untreated for some time first make an appointment to see a cranial sacral osteopath or chiropractor to make sure you know what the problem is and receive a treatment to help your body relieve the pressure immediately. Acupuncture is also an excellent antidote to relieving the pain and re-directing the general flow of energy.

However, your body may have a strong habitual holding pattern that causes the condition to return even after therapy and it is therefore essential that you have a self-help exercise program to maintain a healthy posture. As with scoliosis of the spine, practicing yoga regularly should be your mainstay, but also swimming on your back, doing back crawl is an excellent and gentle way of opening up those channels of energy and releasing pressure. Combining stretch and relaxation are the elements you need to heal this condition.

The health of your kidneys and adrenal glands can also influence the sciatic nerve and visa versa, so if you do have a tendency to sciatica keeping your lower back, neck and feet warm during the winter is very important to maintain good circulation and boost your energy.

Again drinking plenty of water throughout the day re-constitutes your whole system giving your nerves the hydration required to function at optimum levels of calm efficiency.

Useful Remedies and Blends
When your hands, wrists or indeed any part of you feel strained or imbalanced the use of aromatic oils and homeopathic remedies can be of great assistance. The following remedies are designed for their benefits in healing specific imbalance.

Homeopathic Remedies
Arnica – for internal or external bruising, swelling or poor circulation.

Rhus Tox – for chronic pain in your joints and spine.

Ruta – for weakness and sensitivity in the nerves or muscles.

Aromatherapy
To be blended in equal parts in a carrier base oil.
Therapeutic ratio - 10 ml base oil to 10 drops of essential oils
Rosemary, Lavender, Bay – to heal damaged muscular tissue and

improve circulation in muscles and joints

Jasmine, Frankincense, Rose – to calm, de-stress and deepen breathing

Eucalyptus, Clove, Ginger/Tangelo- to reduce pain in the muscles and joints

Blue Chamomile, Sandalwood, Clary Sage – to promote deep relaxation and sleep

Vitamins and Minerals
If you are unsure about taking supplements consult a qualified nutritionist.
Calcium and Magnesium – to strengthen skeletal structure and bones

MSM – to balance nerve pain within the muscles and strengthen muscle tissue

B Complex – for tiredness, low immunity and stress.

Oil of Evening Primrose – to balance hormonal tension and release pressure

Zinc and Vitamin E – for healing wounds, scared tissue and burns.

Feverfew – for migraines and frequent headaches.

Self Massage
The following techniques are drawn from the Do-in tradition of self massage that uses yoga postures and knowledge of the meridian system to balance and relax the body. The principle of the techniques is that the body is supported and in repose, the muscles slightly stretched so that you can reach them easily.

Lower Back Beat
This can be done with a blend of oils or over clothing and is excellent for relaxing the lower lumbar muscles and boosting kidney energy to release excess adrenalin and stress.

Kneel on the floor and bring your head down as if in Childs Pose

You can use a pillow under your forehead to help relax your

neck.

Make fists with your hands

Place the back of your fists either side of the base of your spine

Begin to beat firmly (not too hard) up and down either side of the spinal column as high as your hands will reach, up and down about 20 times

Then place your palms, hands down, on the sacral area and smooth outwards toward the hips six times.

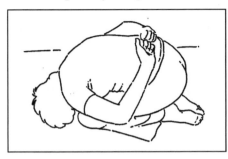

If you are using oils to relax the lower back muscles, massage around the lower back and hips in broad circular strokes, stretching downwards.

Then lie on your back with a pillow under your knees to relax.

Neck Stretch Massage

Kneeling in the same posture as above, in Childs Pose, with a cushion beneath your forehead.

Smooth any hair away from the back of your neck

Apply some aromatherapy oils on your fingertips and stroke into the back of your neck.

Then with alternating hands stroke slowly and firmly from the seventh cervical vertebrae up toward the occipital ridge, stretching the neck muscles on one side and then the other.

Repeat this alternating neck stretch massage at least 15 times.

Then create circular movements under the occipital ridge.

Now bring your hands down by your sides and let your shoulders and arms relax completely in the Childs Pose.

After a while slowly lift up before your stand or lie down to relax further.

Confident hands – Peaceful hands

Massage techniques may differ but one element common to all is the *quality* of your touch. Your hands speak an aesthetic language that goes beyond the learnt physical techniques to the subtle, intuitive aspect of your awareness. Even to your soul. No matter how skilled you are the essence of communicating any technique lies deep within you, in the natural sense you have of where your touch is coming from, and how it actually feels. It can be helpful to imagine that it is you on the couch. What messages are being transmitted through your touch? How would you like to be touched? How would you like to feel about your therapist? What are your hands saying?

If you feel insecure, your client will feel unsure of you.

Primary hand care

Within this book you will find many keys to help you develop more confidence in your hands but the following tips are vital ingredients to further nourish the quality of how your hands feel. Remember, this is a two way street, so you will reap the benefits just as much as your client.

Scrub your hands with salts and oils on a regular basis. This purifies them and maintains a sublimely soft texture to your skin.

Keep nails clean and short enough to be able to carry out deep tissue massage when required. Don`t let long nails scare your client!

On first contact with your client just let your hands rest peacefully on their back, feet, abdomen or head before you begin to massage.

Let go of any tension in your shoulders, arms, elbow and wrists allowing your hands to deeply relax on their body. Do not apply pressure – just a relaxed contact.

This introduces your energy and touch to the client, initiating their receptivity.

A relaxed soft touch will instil confidence and trust from you to your client.

Simply be aware of the touch of your relaxed hands and breathe.

As you work through this handbook you will naturally integrate deepening techniques of breathing and energy balancing into the quality and effectiveness of your touch.

Couch Comfort
As we discussed earlier in this chapter your couch set-up and height will help support you at a fundamental level of therapeutic benefit. Equally your client, who may be on the couch for over one hour at a time, needs to feel comfortable along the same principles as you do. Therefore, sufficient and correctly placed support bolsters, cushions and towels are essential for balance and warmth.

Always check with your client that they want the support your suggest if you are not sure.

Couch support options when client is resting face down.
Face cradle to align the neck and spine and prevent unnecessary twisting of muscles and joints.

Bolster support under the ankles to relax the angle of the feet, knees and lower back muscles.

For large breasted women they may need a folded towel wedged under the rib-cage or directly under the breasts, to help reduce pressure on the chest.

People with limited mobility in the shoulders or arms may need arm rest supports attached beneath the level of the couch.

Those will chronic lower back pain may need large cushions or bolsters placed under the hips to raise the sacral area and reduce pressure from the spine.

Couch support options when client is resting face up
Bolster placed under the knees to relax the lower back muscles and spine.

Or some may prefer the bolster under the ankles for the same reason.

For those with a very tense of stiff neck place a cushion or large folded towel under the head.

Those with arthritic arms or very tight shoulders may need folded towels under the forearm to relax the wrists, elbows and shoulders.

Checking the Sagital Plane

In addition to the above supports for your client always check and observe their body alignment when lying on the couch. The following techniques will give you both more balance to work with.

Face down Body Alignment

When lying face down make sure their hips are balanced and the legs and feet are resting apart. To adjust lift the legs gently at the ankles and slowly swing the legs a little distance from side to side, until the balance is corrected. Then place the legs down about 2 ft apart

Observe the shoulders and go to the head of the couch and place one hand on each of their shoulders. Gently rock and push the shoulders down from side to side, then hold both with a soft downwards pressure for a few seconds.

Now stand to the side of the couch and place one hand at the base of the spine, one hand on the sacral area and your other hand between the shoulder blades. With your fingertips and heel of hand touching either side of the spinal column, rock gently to and fro a few times. Then just hold to calm the nervous energy around the spine.

Face up Body Alignment

When the client is face up observe that their hips are balanced, legs straight and apart. Take a hold of the heels and lifting the legs just a few inches from the couch swing the legs slowly from side to side to adjust the angle of the hips.

Observe the feet and toes and to align and balance stroke down the inside of the calf muscle to the sole of the foot. Holding one foot in each hand pull the legs a little towards you and then let them down to the couch. Then gently push down into the arch area of feet, rocking from side to side and stroke off the big toe.

Observe the shoulders and standing at the head of the couch place one hand on each shoulder. Gently apply a little pressure and rock from side to side pushing the shoulders down and hold for a few seconds.

Observe the angle of the neck and head and placing your hands under the neck stroke up through the neck, gently pulling up through the back of the head. Cradle and hold the head slowly rolling it from side to side and then balance it down to the couch at the centre, carefully sweeping your hands out from beneath.

Super Body Breaks - Exercises

They take just a few minutes and can save you hours of stress.....
At the end of a session if you feel really zapped try these Super Body Breaks to help your body let go and free itself from any blockages or imbalance.

Tai-chi spinal twists
Stand with your legs at least 3 feet apart with feet turned out and knees bent outwards.

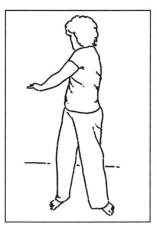

Swing your upper body and arms all the way to the right and then to the left.

Make sure your neck and head turn with your arms and look behind you.

Let your arms be really loose and relaxed as if they don't belong to you.

Breathe In as you swing right

Breathe Out as you swing left.

Swing side to side without stopping doing between 6 to 12 turns each side.

Upper body hang-out

Stand and stretch your arms up to the ceiling and hold that stretch for a minute or so.

Then slowly bend all the way forward towards the floor bending your knees slightly to protect your lower back.

When you are completely bent over straighten your legs and let your arms, neck and head just hang loose.

Roll your shoulders round a few times.

Nod your head up and down a few times.

Then simply hang there for a 1 - 3 minutes, breathing and letting go.

Imagine tensions are rolling down your back, shoulders and arms dripping off your fingertips away from you.

Then bending your knees, **come up slowly squeezing your buttocks** to protect your lower back.

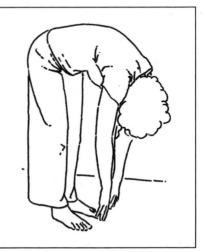

Instant back repair

Place a towel or mat on the floor and a cushion that goes under both knees.

Lie flat on your back on the floor with the cushion placed under your knees.

Pull one knee in towards your chest grasping with both hands, whilst raising the other leg a few inches off the floor and point the toe.

Breathe in and pull the knee firmly to your chest.

Breathe out and lift your head to your knee.

Hold for 6 seconds breathing freely.

Then relax head and leg down to the floor.

Repeat with other leg. Do each side 3 x.

Take a deep breath in and squeeze your buttocks and abdominal muscles in, holding for 5 seconds.

Release and relax.

Roll onto your left side and push yourself up from the side angle.

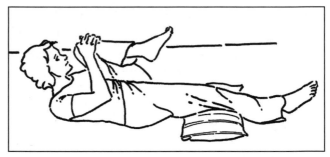

Hand and wrist mobility

Massage oils around the carpal bones in your wrists and around the base of your thumbs and stretch the muscles up your forearms to your elbows.

Then simply rotate your hands and wrists round in circles in both directions.

Press both hands together then with open fingers press the fingers against each other, slightly bending them backwards.

Shoulder release

Stand with yours hands and fingers interlocked behind your back.

Bend slowly forward from the waist and bring your arms as far up behind you as possible, rotating the shoulders

As you hang down gently pull back with your shoulders and let your head hang loose.

Breathe and relax for 6 – 12 counts.

Bend your knees and slowly come up to a straight spine.

Release of your hands letting them hang loosely by your sides.

Shake your hands and wrists out.

See picture for Wrist, Hand and Shoulder Release Two

Prepare your body – free your mind
Body maintenance tips

Like any athlete you do need to keep training your body in such a way that you maintain core strength, stamina and overall good health.

Here are a few tips and guidelines on how to keep your self physically fit for the job.

Exercise regularly

Exercise at least twice a week in such a way that you not only generate good cardio vascular activity, but also release the build up of lactic acids from the muscular tissue and joints. The exercises that stretch you in this way and also help to re-align your body are yoga, swimming, long walks, tai-chi and pilates when practiced on a regular basis. The movements within these forms help cleanse your body of toxins, create better flexibility, deepen your breathing, rotate the joints and stretch out the muscles. These exercises also work with the circulation of more subtle energy helping you to let-go of the accumulation of physical tensions and how they may affect your total well-being.

Core strength exercises

Your core strength is housed in the grounding and centring power of the 'hara', the connecting space between your first and second chakras (subtle energy centres). These energy centres are located in your lower abdominal area and base of your spine. The abdomen relates to the storing of reusable energy behind the naval that recharges your inner battery and resources of vital energy. The dynamic pull of magnetic grounding energy from your root chakra at the coccyx balances your connection with the earth and brings fresh energy up through your legs and spine. These chakras are further elaborated on in the chapter Your Spirit.

Developing the physical element of your Core Strength can be easily accomplished with basic exercises that develop your muscles in these areas, supporting a more subtle circulation of energy.

Lie flat on your back on a mat on the floor and bend your knees, keeping your feet touching the floor.

Basic Core Strength Exercise One

Inhale and pull the abdominal muscles firmly inwards as if you were trying to bring your abdomen to touch your spine. Hold for 5 seconds

Exhale and release the hold and while the breath is out pull the abdominal muscles in again. Hold for 5 seconds.

Repeat the above in cycles of 3.

Basic Core Strength Exercise Two

Inhale and draw your buttock muscles inwards as tightly as you can. Hold for up to 5 seconds.

Exhale and whilst the breath is out draw the buttock muscles in again. Hold for 5 seconds.

Repeat the above in cycles of 3 alternating with Exercise 1

The following yoga poses also help develop your core strength when practiced regularly.

Receive a body work session

Make sure you receive body therapy yourself on a regular basis. Not only does this help to de-stress your muscles and joints, but it continues to develop your awareness of how techniques actually feel and is always a learning experience. You become the receiver which reminds you about the internal processes that can arise. Remember that you, your body and mind, are changing all the time and this will put you in touch with new sensations you may not be aware of. This is food for your body and nourishment for your soul; a way of rewarding yourself with the joys of receiving that which you are giving. This is a direct sensory and silent experience that develops your insight and skill on a deeply instinctual level, naturally enriching your ability to give and experience the benefits of deep relaxation.

Helpful yoga poses for release, strength and balance

Sun Salutations (3x) Practice at the beginning of each day to open up your energy, release static and avoid building up tensions. Follow the movements one after the other as smoothly as you can, breathing deeply. You can hold each pose for two or three breaths and always complete the salutation with hands at the heart centre as shown. Close your eyes, be aware of your heart-beat and feet beneath you, breathe and relax.

Sitting Warrior Pose Bringing one arm up behind the head and reaching down between the shoulders. Pull the elbow back with your other hand then release it to reach behind your back aiming for your upper hand. You can use a strap between your hands to bring them closer together. Repeat on both sides.

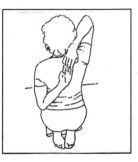

Crow Pose- Squatting, letting your lower back sink to the floor. Breathe and hold for a few minutes if you can.

Camel Pose – Kneeling with a back bend, hands on the floor or on

the heels supporting you from behind. Stretch back, relax your neck as much as you can, breathe and look up. Hold for a few deep breaths then practice Childs Pose.

Childs Pose Kneeling into a full forward bend to the floor.

Supine Twist Lying on back on the floor, bend one leg and the place foot on the other knee, and stretch your other arm above your head. Then twist that knee and leg towards the floor rotating the hip. Breathe and hold for a minute then slowly come back to centre and repeat on the other side.

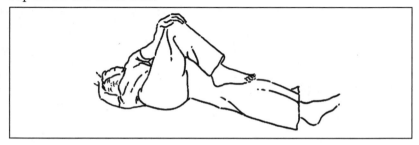

Maltese Cross Lying on your back with arms out to the sides at shoulder height and legs together flat on the floor. Lift your right leg up to 90 degree angle from the floor and then take it across your body aiming for your left hand.

Take a hold of the foot or ankle if you can reach and just breathe, stretching and relaxing that leg as much as possible.

Then slowly bring the leg back up to centre and return to the floor.

Now lift your left leg up 90 degrees and take it across your body to the right hand or floor. Hold as above. Repeat this three times on both sides.

Embryo Lying on the back, lifting the head and hugging both knees to your chest to relax and round the lower back and vertebrae.

Savassana – is a state of deep relaxation following yoga asanas. Lying flat on your back on the floor, legs at least two feet apart, palms upward facing with your thumb and index finger gently touching and eyes softly closed. Allow your body to completely let go into the surface, breathing and relaxing. During savassana people often drift off into the theta state, described in Deep Relaxation below.

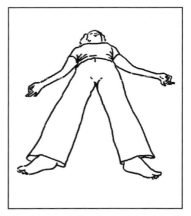

Deep Relaxation Therapy

The concept of deep relaxation as a therapeutic experience within itself has become more and more pertinent as stress levels rise. You and your spa client are greatly supported in total health and wellbeing by understanding the principles and practices that lead to a deeply relaxed state of mind. Learning how to access a depth of relaxation can be achieved through yoga and that is certainly what the experience of savassana gives. However, deep levels of relaxation that bring the body and the mind into a super-relaxed awareness can be created through many other routes. The principle of deep relaxation therapy is to create Theta Waves.

The brain is known to produce a chemical-electrical energy and there are four researched categories of brain waves that the human brain generates. Our everyday mind, that is engaged in an activity of active concentration, analysis, action or debate will generate Beta Waves which also relate to cognitive thinking. Beta waves move at a rate of 15-40 cycles per second and reveal a strongly engaged mind. When the mind begins to slow down, perhaps through just sitting and taking a break, walking, reflecting, perhaps even watching TV, Alpha Waves are generated which are a slower frequency of energy that move at a rate of between 9-14 cycles per second. This shows signs of the brain disengaging and retreating a little in some way

Theta Waves are the next level of slowing down brain activity and are related to a sense of detachment from physical reality in one form or another. The frequency range moves between 5-8 cycles per second, a marked shift down from the alpha state. The electrical energy creating theta waves comes from a sense of time lost, or timelessness or elevation, where the mind drifts off, and is not aware of the physical body yet retains a level of sensory awareness. Out of this theta state of mind often arise great new ideas, or realisations yet the other thoughts around that idea, or where they came from in terms of linear thinking are not known or remembered in a cognitive way. Ideas and reflections flow freely during this repose, without censorship or guilt, and is therefore a very positive, healing frame of mind.

Daydreaming, deep meditation, long motorway driving, running, massage, spa bathing and other repetitive movements where the body is somehow forgotten or at rest, when the mind is free to roam are common situations that generate these brain waves. The Theta state serves to create a deeply regenerative and creative internal environment of well-being. The growth in environmentally harmonious music, guided relaxations, visuali-sation and meditations are working towards generating this altered state. Pain relief clinics use deep relaxation therapy, progressive muscular relaxation, meditation, visualization and breathing techniques to therapeutically change the sufferers relationship with pain, disassociating from it and thereby reducing the painful symptoms.

For your own well-being the theta state is an optimum quality of mind to experience over and over again. It allows for a deeper process of letting go of stress and tension on the level of the body-mind relationship, which is the interface where most resistance and tension is held. As in the creation of theta waves, it is also repeating the practices that create this state that matures your ability to reach deeper levels of relaxation. You can take time out to practice your ability to go into this state rather than just hoping it will happen spontaneously, though it may. Practicing yoga, breathing and meditation etc are all effective ways to slow down the brain waves and come into this elevated space. Today there are even technologies that create pulses designed to alter brain rhythms that directly affect nerve centres and the brain-waves.

The spa environment is designed to initiate this process of unwinding the tight coils in the body-mind relationship and after a thorough spa experience of bathing, steaming, sauna, cold showers or plunge pools the mind is often brought into an altered state whereby people can relax and drift off completely. As a therapist, when you treat your client with deeply relaxing aromatic oils, harmonious massage and chakra energy balancing, you are also influencing the electro-chemical responses in the brain thereby creating the potential for a theta experience.

The fourth level of brain waves, Delta Waves, are generated during sleep and are of the greatest amplitude but the slowest frequency of between 1.5 and 4 cycles per second. In the deepest dreamless sleep the brain can be at the lowest frequency of 2, and the brain dead mind is registered at 0. During deep sleep dreaming is known to occur in 90 minute cycles and raises the frequency so that REM, rapid eye movement, occurs.

Progressive muscular relaxation exercise

This well-tried and tested form of tension release for the body also benefits the mind. The chemistry of breathing deeply combined with physical tension release creates a calming internal environment that is just the right equation to enter sleep with a lighter spirit. Practice at the end of a busy day to consciously unwind and sleep peacefully.

Simply lying on your back you tense and release all the different muscle groups, in succession from your feet to the top of your head, with deep breaths. Repeating the whole body process twice is advised.

For example

Breathe in and point your toes, holding tension in your feet.

Hold this for 5 seconds.

Then exhale through your mouth and letting the tension go and wait 5 seconds.

Breathe in and flex your feet up pushing the claves into the floor.

Hold for 5 seconds, then exhale powerfully and let the feet relax for 5 seconds.

In the same way breathe and tense all the major muscle groups, thighs, lower back , abdomen, chest, hands, arms, shoulders, neck, face.

On completion simply deeply relax and wake up refreshed for a new day.   —

Cleansing your body

After a day of body- work you need to cleanse and refresh your skin. Don`t sleep on the days energy – wash it away. The process of spa treatments naturally shed dead skin cells as well as basic body `malas` from your clients. A Mala is the ayurvedic term for the waste-matter that the body is constantly eliminating in the form of hair, nails, skin, gases, perspiration, mucous, exhalation, sweat, urine and faeces. Always shower or bath before you go to bed to help your body purify itself from the energy of the day. Use a loofer or brush to remove your own dead skin cells and generate a rigorous sense of renewal that also improves lymph drainage and circulation. Cleansing opens the pores and allows your skin to breathe enabling your *electro magnetic field* to diffuse any of the`dross`, the accumulation of static or debilitating vibrations you may have picked up.

The electro magnetic field will be further discussed in Key Number Four Your Spirit.

Sleeping peacefully

Sleep is the heavenly renewing environment where we are given the space to replenish and recharge ourselves in the sanctity of bed. If the pressures and demands of the day have built up a residue of excess tensions and thoughts, it is vital to off load a measure of this before you go to sleep so that you are not processing too much of it in your dreams. The discussion on Deep Relaxation will be helpful for you.

Stay hydrated

Water is the singular fluid that does a multitude of good, seeping its way into every atom of your being - literally. As you know our biological make-up is at least 75% water and this substance is one of the vital resources we need to replenish in order to access our infinite power of energy. It is easy to forget to drink when you are busy but just make sure that after EVERY session you drink at least one glass of water. This not only replaces the fluids keeping you hydrated, but also helps to flush out any toxicity or tension you may accumulate. Water is also your basic life giving food source that flows where other things cannot reach. Do not underestimate the power of water.

In addition water helps to bring fresh oxygen into your body and mind recharging your batteries and purifying your system of excess carbons that can cause headaches, heaviness and digestive problems.

Personal Profiling through Ayurvedic Governing Elements

Ayurvedic philosophy is rooted in the understanding of knowing which elements govern all living things and therefore the human body, mind and emotions. The five elements of earth, air, fire, water and space are categorised into three main 'types' called the Tri Dosha. Each one of us is composed of all the elements yet our fundamental constitution reveals that we all have a predominant element that influences every area of our life. Ayurveda seeks to address the tendency to be too strong in one element that may weaken the other elements required to lead a balanced, healthy life. Through raising your self-awareness and making the correct lifestyle choices as well as food and exercise you can redress this balance.

Ayurveda means 'Science of Life' and offers vast and in-depth therapeutic diagnostic and healing practices that include purification rituals, nutrition and herbal medicine, massage, yoga and meditation.

Discover your Dosha

Use the chart below to identify which **Dosha** in each **Condition** you resemble.

If you find it difficult to identify which dosha in each category resembles you most, Kapha, Pitta or Vatta that is quite common as many people are a combination of two dosha.

It this is the case write them both down with the strongest dosha first.

For example in the category 'Temperament' may have kapha and pitta tendencies, so write them both down with the strongest dosha first.

When you have completed them all add up the **majority** of the **strongest dosha** to see which type you are. You may score say six kapha and three pitta. This means that your predominant dosha is kapha with secondary pitta tendencies. The one with the most points is your **predominat dosha** and therefore your **key governing element**.

If it is an even 50/50 split between two dosha, then go with what YOU think is most appropriate at this time. The body is often in flux and change, and conditions such as your age, stress levels, work environment and how you take care of yourself will influence the balance of your elements.

THE THREE DOSHA – TRI DOSHA

CONDITIONS	KAPHA	PITTA	VATTA
Governing elements	Earth/Water	Fire/Water	Air/space
Physical traits	Large build/ compact	Medium build	Long/ narrow build
Structure	Balanced/ grounded	Average/ energetic	Tall or petite
Temperament	Steady/romantic/ honest	Motivated/ passionate	Sociable/ quick
Skin - generally	Oily to congested	Normal to changeable	Dry to sensitive
Skin problems	Blocked pores/ spots/milia	Pimples/acne/ rosacea	Dehydrated/ sensitive/ psoriasis
Body tendencies	Sluggish circulation/ lymph	Over acidity/ indigestion	Excess gasses/poor breathing

UNDER STRESS

Emotional Imbalance	Depressed/tearful/ tire	Irritable/ demanding/ argues	Avoids feelings/ insecure
Physical Imbalance	Poor circulation/ elimination	Digestive problems/IBS	Skeletal weaknes/joint pain
Psychological Imbalance	Stubborn/quiet	Impateint/ critical/angry	Erratic/ unfocused/ non-commital

Knowing your predominat dosha will help you to make the right choices in balancing yourself. Here are a few tips that can open the door to your interest and in Ayurveda and restore vital energy levels.

Rebalancing Tips

Kapha	Pitta	Vatta
Enjoy Yoga, tai-chi, singing	Walk in nature, meditate by water	Reflect, visualise, be still, alone
Avoid Wheat, dairy foods, meat	Spicy, acidic foods and coffee	Pulses, potatoes, citrus fruits
Eat Berries,lemons,greens	Yoghurt,yams,soya products	Avocados, melons,fish

Food source

You are what you eat and you simply can't get away from the fact that good food is the fuel that gives us longevity and life. But does the food you eat simply fill the gap or give you the benefit of excellent health and a 'lightness of being', so necessary for the therapist?

Where time is of the essence during your breaks its easy to opt for the quick fix satisfaction of fast food sources, rather than thinking ahead and planning a little with getting nourishing alternatives. If you eat stoge you will feel 'stoggey,' your system becoming congested and constipated. If you consume too much stimulating food your system will become taxed and acidic causing stress and corrosion of your vital organs. If you consume heavy foods on a regular basis you will become heavy and over-tired and not able to sustain a more sensitive balance. Toxic foods, gain weight, block your system, cloud your thinking and drain your energy. *Don't do it!*

Besides being a great source of nourishment food is also a great source of comfort, joy, energy and healing. And for the therapist at work you need to make sure that your body is getting exactly what it needs to sustain you on all levels. Nutrition is a vast subject, constantly being researched and you can find out a great deal more from the huge resource of literature on this interesting subject. Most therapists have a good knowledge of what is good for you and how to you use it.. but often when we get out of balance we forget how important good nutrition is. Also, our bodies are changing all of the time and therefore our needs on a biological, chemical and energetic level need to be reviewed.

If you think your digestion or energy is not up to parr, or you have developed some allergies to foods do go and see a qualified Nutritionist who can give you valuable advice and insight on how to upgrade yourself.

However, the following basic but fundamental guidelines are specifically given to help you, the therapist, energise, sustain and heal yourself during your working day.

Breakfast
Don't miss it! Set up your digestive system with slow burning fuel that will nourish you through the morning and help you stay strong and relaxed. This also prevents your blood sugar levels from dropping by 11 am!

Porridge and oat-based cereal

Soya products

Eggs and whole meal toast

Hhoney, yoghurts, seeds

Protein drinks

Fresh fruits of all kinds can all set you up well for the day ahead.

Avoid – fried foods, sugar and coffee with breakfast.

Morning snacks
Nuts, raisins, nut/fruit bars, dried fruit.

Bananass, apples, apricots and peaches.

Fruit juices.

Green tea, Red Bush Tea, Ginseng Tea,

Miso soup drink

Organic Coffee – if you drink coffee best to have a small cup 2-3 times a day rather than one huge fix... This will help your body to use the caffeine efficiently and not over-tax your kidneys which are the vital organs that generates natural 'chi' energy through your system.

Lunch

Make it light! Too much food of any description will cause a lot of blood to rush to your stomach to digest it, taking vital energy away from your muscles and brain. You will also feel very tired and weak in the afternoon. Try small portions of....

Bean salads
Light fish or tofu sandwiches
Avocados
All kinds of salads
Raw vegeatables
Pasta
Sushi
Hot soup with small amount of bread
Fruit and vegetable juices
Avoid – heavy meat, pastries, pies, potatoes, fried food, too much bread, too much cheese or cooked food.

Afternoon snacks

Teas as above
Organic Green and Black chocolate (a little)
Nuts and seeds
Dried Fruit
Fruit juice
These also help to keep you blood sugar levels up without blasting yourself with stimulants.
And wWater water water

Vitamins and supplements

This again is a vast subject and can be very specific to each person. If you think your body is seriously under performing you may need extra vitamins and minerals to support you. Constant colds, pain in your joints, regular headaches and poor digestion may all be symptoms of poor nutrition. Please consult a Nutritionist to advise you. Make sure that any supplements you take are from a 'food source' derivative which makes them easier and cleaner to digest and assimilate.

Your Body Clock

The body clock is drawn from an oriental model of holistic medicine that treats the body through the meridian system, like acupressure, acupuncture and Chinese herbal medicine. In the same way that ayurveda is rooted in understanding of the governing elements of Tri-dosha, so oriental medicine has two known elements, yin and yang. These are associated respectively, with female and male energies. The body clock is an interesting and helpful frame of reference to integrate into your own well-being, as well as providing insight for your client at time of treatment. Review the cycle on the chart given here.

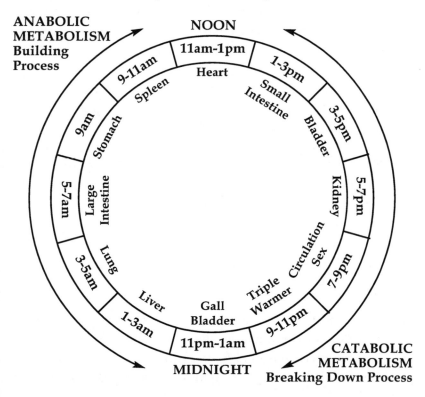

7 – 9 am - **Stomach** – Digestive juices are at their optimum power. This is the best time to eat food that takes a long time to break down e.g., grains. Breakfast in important.

9 – 11 am – **Spleen** – This has a lot to do with the breakdown of sugars and also with our psyche and intellect. This is a good time for in-depth treatments, study, receiving and giving information and guidance. We have more organisational energy at this time.

11 – 1 pm – **Heart** – This is a social time good for meetings, walking, exercise and healing for the heart and circulatory system.

1 – 3 pm – **Small Intestine** – This relates to the break down of food. All heavy meals should be eaten by 2pm for maximum absorption and efficiency. Elimination is boosted at this time.

3 – 5 pm – **Bladder** – Purification of bodily fluids occurring, bladder is very active and an important time to drink plenty of water.

5 – 7 pm – **Kidneys** – In Chinese medicine kidneys relate to vital energy as well as grief and sadness. Eat lightly, practice yoga, mediation, relaxation, bathing, aromatherapy.

7 – 9 pm –**Circulation and Sex Meridian** – A good time to be intimate, share with a lover, family and friends, dance, listen to music, be entertained.

9 – 11 pm - **Triple Warmer** – The body is naturally slowing down, breaking down of the day's fuel and energy, requiring deep relaxation and rest.

11 pm – 1 am – **Gall Bladder** – Toxic waste on every level rises at this time, nausea, anxiety, tensions and worry can arise. Comfort and sleep are important restoring energies.

3 – 5 am – **Lungs** – The lungs are at their optimum now so dreaming can be very vivid. Asthma attacks can happen at this time especially if dreams lead to anxiety. This can also be a time of very insightful and deep sleep.

5 - 7 am **Large Intestine** – The body is ready to eliminate waste and move around, becoming lighter and more energised.

CHAPTER TWO

KEY NUMBER TWO

YOUR BREATHING

The breath is the bridge between your body and your mind
J T Herron

Have you ever noticed how your thinking is reflected in your breathing patterns which act just like a barometer? Notice how nervous, angry or anxious thoughts will speed up your breathing, whereas relaxed, pleasant or peaceful thoughts will slow your breathing down.

This potent relationship between your thoughts, emotion and breath patterns is also true in reverse. When you purposefully deepen and slow your breathing down, your thoughts and feelings will begin to calm and relax. Your breath is at the pivot of your body mind relationship.

The breath and life itself can be seen as one undivided experience. It is your link to the environment and to your consciousness, a trusty friend who is always there for you. It is the most transformative tool you have, completely free and available at all times.

Breathing not only generates the power of your lungs to function, it also recharges the electrical currents in and around your body, fuelling the interactive flow of life energy. This process enables your brain to think, the power of your heart to beat, circulating blood and giving life to all your organs. You know that without the ability to breathe in the oxygen freely available (at least for now!) you would not be able to function.

In this chapter you will learn how to befriend your breath and make it an invaluable therapeutic partner.

Body Mind and Breath

Throughout our lives habitual ways of breathing, stemming from many different causes can directly affect our wellbeing. Active and passive smoking, prescribed or recreational drugs, long term stress or illness, poor nutrition, air pollution, poor posture and allergies, can all adversely affect how you breathe. Psycho-somatic imbalances such as asthma, anxiety, and panic attacks are all characterised by shortness of breath showing clearly how breathing is influenced by our emotional and psychological states.

As we are rarely taught how to breathe correctly, unhealthy breathing habits are common. Many people tend to breathe only into the upper lung and sometimes through the mouth instead of the nostrils. This poor quality of breathing bypasses the physiological inner structure that has naturally evolved to nourish and balance your whole system. Over time, if shallow or restricted breathing continues, this can trigger emotional and physical distress manifesting as serious chronic health conditions.

The body and mind are short changed by shallow breathing which weakens vitality and energy levels creating many common health problems such as high blood pressure, heart disease, headaches, IBS, insomnia, nervous tension and depression, to name just a few of the endless list of associated conditions.

Many of these symptoms are caused by the acid levels present in the blood. If the body does not exhale sufficiently with each breath, the build up of acids and carbons begin to crystallize causing congestion, restriction and tension in the most susceptible areas at the time. By exhaling fully we release excess toxins and stale air which helps the nervous system to relax, benefiting all corresponding parts.

Dr Peter Nixon, a leading heart surgeon from the UK, taught that hyper-ventilation and shallow breathing contributes to almost every phase of heart disease, from the narrowing of the coronary arteries through to the destruction of heart tissue, and ultimately to the triggering of a full-blown heart attack! He is known to treat his patients by examining the exhaled breath for the correct acid-alkaline balance, teaching them breathing techniques to correct and heal symptoms preventing the conditions from occurring again.

Alchemy of the Breath

The magic of breathing deeply is all embracing, creating a chemistry that, as we have seen, balances the acid and alkaline levels within your blood, which is so vital to a healthy body and mind. All forms of tension, whether caused by stress, injury, poor posture, anger, jealousy, anxiety or frustration can promote high levels of acidity that form `crystals` or aggregates of congestion that get lodged in the muscles, connective tissue and joints.

Breathing deeply and breath awareness exercises create an alkaline response in the blood and therefore help to dissolve the acid levels of stress and detoxify the congested crystals. This is turn helps the body balance by manufacturing more alkalinity throughout the body and mind restoring better overall health and well-being.

Body- based therapies also help to open up and relax the body, deepening the breath which increases the circulation throughout the body and mind inducing calming and detoxifying benefits.

The Passage of your Breath

By breathing deeply through your nostrils vital nutrients and oxygen are taken into the full capacity of the lungs and diaphragm via the throat, then the windpipe, and finally to the bronchi in the right and left lung. The lungs then give up the oxygen to the red blood cells which carry it throughout your whole body depositing the oxygen as it goes. During this journey toxic waste in the form of carbon dioxide is picked up by the blood which you then is exhaled out when the blood returns to the lungs.

The exhalation is equally, if not more important than the inhalation. Shallow breathing is often characterised by the inability to exhale fully which obviously limits the successful completion of the breaths journey.

Awakening the Breath

Your nose also serves as an air filtering system in the form of tiny nostril hairs which catch some of the dust particles and other pollutants, preventing them from entering your body. Breathing through the nose stimulates a variety of important responses. Your sense of smell, for example, is a primal survival instinct, which can trigger emotional states that informs us of likes and dislikes, possible danger and pleasurable experiences. This sense of smell is located in the frontal lobe of the brain which contains the *limbic system* that also stores our short and long term memory and other survival instincts such as thirst, hunger, sexual drives and registering of pain.

This limbic system plays a vital role in the emotional connection and awareness we have with our bodies and consequently our empathy for others. Controlled nostril breathing can open up the nerve pathways to this limbic area, tapping into our cellular memory, releasing hidden associations between the body and mind which may be suppressed for any number of reasons.

When deep breathing exercises are intensely practiced over time the stimulation can release forgotten memories that may have pleasant or unpleasant associations. However, all serve to unlock the unconscious reactions we may have to situations in our lives, that could be limiting our potential to see and experience life afresh.

This forgetfulness, or disassociation, may be due to negative or fearful memories, perhaps quite complex, that create an unconscious barrier, blocking access to that feeling again. The danger of this is that the feeling can remain buried in our minds, festering away unconsciously, eventually affecting the health of the body. Or forgetfulness may be due to levels of toxicity and congestion blocking the adequate circulation of breath.

Correct breathing can transform our lives, awakening and inspiring us to a new relationship between our mind and emotions. This is a natural, gentle and liberating process that automatically heals and enriches our self-awareness.

The correct flow of breath into the nasal passages helps to balance the right and left hemispheres of the brain generating more clarity and enlightening our inner perceptions. A natural consequence of correct breathing is a heightened sensitivity and a deepening spontaneous, self-awareness.

Your Abdominal Brain

The power of deep breathing directly accesses what is referred to as your 'abdominal brain' or 'hara' the energy centre discussed in 'Your Body.' Located within the region of your navel there is an intricate network of nerves which influence the management of our energy resources on a physical as well as subtle level. This centre acts like a battery that stores and accumulates energy for future use, recharging your body and mind, and sustaining you during times of stress. It is also a reservoir of important memories that can dramatically colour experience.

Your abdominal brain has direct physical links with the navel 'belly button' (hara) which carries the memory of separation from your mother via the umbilicus. This energy centre responds with powerful spontaneity to emotional stimuli throughout our lives. This is the place where our `gut feelings` are born and the instinctual responses that seem to have no rational association yet we know these feelings are right! The hara connects us to our genetic and karmic memory, creating physical sensations and emotional feelings through our inherent psycho-physiology.

During times of stress or conflict this centre is often the first place to react, and imbalances that affect our digestion and elimination are well known. Most recently medical research has identified 'abdominal migraines' which are common in children whose mental faculties are not as developed as most adults. Medical studies of these conditions have shown that these migraines are triggered by agitated nerves which generate a hyper-acidity in the bloodstream disturbing the delicate chemical balance.

The Journey of your Breath

To be conscious or aware of the passage of the breath as it flows through you is to initiate an open relationship with what you *really* feel and sense. We can purposefully propel the breath into parts of ourselves that need energy or healing, bringing more life there. If you knock your toe or hurt yourself, your immediate response will be to suck in air and hold your toe and breath whilst focusing on the place of pain. You then blow that breath out forcefully only to suck it carefully back in. This is how we channel energy to that injury to both placate it and release the pain. This same principle can be applied in various ways and on many levels including emotionally and psychologically.

The breath is the only involuntary function that you can voluntarily control!

On an emotional level if we do not want to get in touch with a feeling of sadness or embarrassment, for example, we tend to breathe with shallow reluctant breaths so that we can skirt the issue of feeling. We avoid the feeling, toughening up around it! We are trying to distance or separate ourselves from the feeling in the hope it will go away. This speaks for itself, as separation or toughening up clearly implies building up tension to block out too much sensitivity.

The crying breath

Crying is a spontaneous outburst of emotion that often allows the breath to `access all areas` where we inhale powerfully and exhale just as powerfully.

A good `uncontrollable` cry can serve us well in the letting go and healing process, as it is a state whereby we are feeling something so profoundly that it overwhelms our control mechanism and `toughening up` strategies. Crying takes us beyond the mind of reason or analysis into pure experience allowing us the opportunity to touch base with what we really feel. And there, in the midst of total feeling we breathe deeply, awakening the senses and freeing up the old patterns for healing and regeneration.

Breathing laughter

And let us not forget laughter! This too draws on enormous amounts of air and prana, to fill your lungs and saturate your body with fresh energy. Laughter therapy has become a well- known practice to overcome depression and other states of inertia due to the exercise that is generated by the lungs and therefore the whole system. Laughter *is* the best medicine!

Your sixth sense

Neuro-scientists continue to research the connection between the complexity of nerve pathways in the lower diaphragm and abdomen with our emotional responses and experiences. This research focuses on the notion that perhaps this connection creates a tangible 'sixth sense', a psychic awareness that acts as an antennae picking up energy on a vibrational level, feeding back information to the brain/mind that can help to protect, predict and therefore prepare us for whatever arises.

This may be seen as intuition or common sense and to some extent it is, but we must not overlook the thousands of years of meditations and yoga practices that purposefully cultivate the awareness of this centre as the source of fulfilling our potential as human beings in body, mind and spirit. When this energy centre is developed it can become a doorway through which we enter into a timelessness and spaciousness that is both comforting and liber- ating. It is this sense of timelessness that perhaps enables our psychic sensory perception, our sixth sense, to move back or forward in time, foreseeing the future and sorting out our relationship with the past, our karma.

Being aware of your breathing can open the doorway into a whole new dimension of sensitivity that links us to important patterns formed in the past that may well be influencing the present. By tuning into the breath in the present we are tilling the ground for the growth of new potential and a better future. The old and the hidden is brought out into the open by the sheer force of the breath pushing waste to the surface and presenting your mind with forgotten feelings or thoughts that need to be re-cycled and released. The breath serves as the fuel enabling the body to be conscious, to change, to grow and to heal.

Healing through the Hara

Consequently, the abdomen is a two edged sword. On the one hand it is an anchor for your breath, storing energy for creative physical use and emotional expression. On the other hand, it becomes the storehouse or 'waste ground' of undigested matter, tired or misdirected energy and associated feelings that can fester and block the healthy circulation of your creativity.

Directing your breath into the hara to transform your energy levels is an essential aspect of this chapter and your effectiveness as a therapist. Your own intimate experience of hara breathing and awareness is fundamental to tuning into your client. Keep in mind the Story of Two.

Many people do not like the hara touched at all during massage, as the awareness that physical touch brings to mind may be too emotionally stimulating for the client to experience at that time. Therefore guiding the breath here is a beneficial and appropriate option for healing. Combining the breath with subtle Energy Balancing is also an effective technique which we will discuss further in the chapter, Your Spirit.

Guiding your client to breathe into this area is a direct, gentle yet powerful way to bring consciousness, release and therefore healing energy to the treatment as a whole. It also serves as a pause for 'integration' so that you and your client can balance body, mind and spirit. **The Integration Breath** Practice later in this chapter will help to guide you both through this process.

Many traditional meditations focus on this centre of energy as the key to inner peace and spiritual awakening.

Prana and Breath

The breath also carries the mysterious yet kinetic qualities of

Prana. Prana is the yogic term for 'vital life energy', comparable to the Chinese term `Chi.` Prana, like Chi, exists within and around all living things yet is not dependent on them. Prana is the energy that sustains the world as we know it, and even perhaps beyond this!

When we inhale oxygen we are also absorbing prana that is directly ingested through the action of the lungs, which are the most physical and dense tools of prana. The most subtle form of prana is in the quality of our thinking and thought processes which we will discuss in the chapter Your Mind. Prana nourishes every aspect of being alive in the body and is vital to our existence whether we realise it or not.

Though prana circulates everywhere regardless of whether you are attuned to it or not, its` more empowering benefits are felt when we consciously connect with the process of breathing. Your awareness enhances the quality of prana and is therefore an important ingredient for the potential healing that lives inside the chemistry of breathing. This is one of the reasons why yoga is such a helpful practice for therapists as all postures are working with the circulation of prana to restore balance and good health.

Pranayama, which are yoga breathing exercises, allow a conscious flow of enriching quantities of prana to reach deeply into the bodily system. Pranayama functions through specific channels or pathways called 'nadis' that are distributed in hundreds throughout the body. There are however, three main pathways that are easily accessed by breathing rhythmically through the left and right nostrils to increase and balance the circulation prana, this life force. Nadis are an intrinsic part of the chakra system discussed in Your Spirit.

If you are not breathing, your client is not breathing

The reason that conscious breathing is essential to you as a body work therapist is because it is at the very core of your relationship with yourself, and hence with your client. Remember that you are the giver in the dynamic of the therapy room so you must lead. *If* *you`re not breathing your client is not breathing.* Remembering this truth can save you from the build up of huge amounts of unnecessary stress and protect you from being drained by the unconscious situations and blind spots.

The rhythms and energy that intermingle between you and your client during the intimacy of a massage, plug you both into each others breath patterns and the strongest pattern can dominate a session, whether for good or not! If you are forgetting to breathe deeply or practice some of the grounding and centring breaths given here you are opening yourself up to perhaps stifling or negative energy. The way you breathe will influence your client one way or another. You will certainly experience an upgraded quality to your sessions when breathing is present. Supporting yourself with breath automatically supports your client.

In discussing the breath here, I have taken a broad and eclectic view of its physical, emotional, psychological and spiritual associations so that you can use it one whatever level you `intend` to. Intention empowers your breathing and is further enriched by using the suggested affirmations and dialogue to bolster its transforming ability as described in Your Mind. Each time you breathe you are inviting life in, desiring to live and explore the nest moment. Make it conscious.

> *'The breath is the bridge between your body and your mind'*
> *J T Herron*

Meditating on the breath

By paying attention to the physical aspects of the breath you will naturally become aware of the more subtle sensations. This dynamic can open up the hidden or buried parts of your self-nature that may have become trapped or submerged in the tension that poor breathing habits create. Your breath is a catalyst that can transform the way you feel, acting like a bridge between your body and mind over which energy and insights can pass.

Each breath is totally new and independent, it lives only for the moment. Every breath you take is a positive decision affirming your intention to live whether this desire is conscious or unconscious you chose it every time you breathe.

Your Life draws insight from deep within the passage of the breath, from that original desire to draw the breath in and re-create new life. From that primal impulse deep within us all to choose life as we inhale our first breath, as we inhale *every* breath and our natural intelligence to let go of what we do not need as we exhale. Life can be experienced as a series of breaths. Each breath is new, original and independent yet is intrinsically linked to each breath that has gone before. Your past, your present, your future lies within the passage of your breath.

Each breath can be a journey, absorbing the experience of the moment and imprinting it in our cellular structure, in our body and mind. The quality of breathing creates an alchemical process influencing the depth at which change occurs. Inhaling, we invite life in to fuel our relationship with all that we experience enabling us to get in touch with the moment.

Exhaling we express a response, an outgoing relationship to what has been taken in or received through the inhalation. Exhaling fully we allow ourselves to let go of surplus or unhealthy residue, creating space for new life and new breath.

And so our lives unfold in the wake of our inner story, chronicled in the breathing patterns and associations that define us.

Breathing exercises for your personal wellbeing

The Essential Stress Release Breath
This excellent exercise is an effective tool to release and recharge your batteries from the hara, your `abdominal brain`. It at once balances your blood from too much acidity, stale air and the build-up of physical tensions as well as giving your body-mind a charge of fresh energy. It is de-stressing, de-toxing and relaxing.

Use it to de-stress, de-tox and relax.

The Practice
Place one hand on your abdomen and one hand on your heart.

Breathe deeply into the abdomen so that your hand rises.
Hold that breath for the count of 4.
Then purse your lips and release the breath in very short puffs.
Pause on empty for 3 counts.
Repeat this cycle from 3 to 6 times.

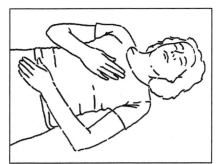

Super Boost Energy Breath
This breath is also known as `Breath Of Fire` and originates from the Kundalini Yoga tradition. It is a dynamic exercise that flushes out blockages on many levels of the body mind relationship, particularly boosting the brain cells through the rapid circulation of blood to the shoulders, neck and head. This is best practiced with closed eyes. It is clearing, uplifting and empowering. A really great start to the day.

Use it when you want to boost your energy, release tension from your shoulders and clear your mind.

The Practice
Sit on the floor using a cushion or kneeling.
Bring your arms out to the sides at a 90 degree angle, palms up.
Inhale and powerfully bring your arms up along side your head.
Then immediately exhale powerfully also through the nose, bringing your arms back to the 90 degree angle.
Continue to rapidly breathe and simultaneously move your arms up and down. Begin with 26 repetitions and work up to 56 repetitions of the breath and movement.
Then just sit peacefully to integrate and be aware of how you feel for a few minutes.
Complete the exercise by breathing deeply into the abdomen, holding the breath for 5 seconds and slowly exhale through the

mouth.

Slowly get up, smile and have a great day.

Breath Awareness Meditation

Focusing on the hara as you breathe is at the core of many traditional meditations that bring you unequivocally back to your centre, into the moment. Practice on a regular basis will cultivate feelings of peace and calm that overflows into your everyday life also benefiting your client. This naturally creates more inner space and resourcefulness that sustains you during times of stress. Practice develops more patience, receptivity and an ability to overcome daily issues which in the past may have frustrated you.

Breath awareness attunes you to your higher mind, enriching your self awareness and consciousness. This strengthens and protects, grounding your presence in the treatment room giving you more confidence and the sensibility to 'hold the space', in the still silence of your work.

Use this powerful breath awareness practice once or twice a day for 15 to 30 minutes or for an hour. The longer the session the deeper you will go into yourself enriching the benefits you will receive. Practice centres you creating a powerful anchor for your mind and emotions. As your practice and concentration develops you will build up a dynamic resource of energy that overflows into everyday life.

You can practice this either lying flat on your back with support under your knees or sitting comfortably with a straight spine. Let your hands lay peacefully at your sides, or on the abdomen or legs.

The Practice
Close your eyes and be aware of the breath flowing into your abdomen.

Begin to breathe in deeply so that your abdomen expands and rises when you inhale.

As you exhale, feel your abdomen fall, relax and empty.

As you inhale think inwardly to yourself, `Rising` ,as you feel the abdomen expand and fill up.

As you exhale think to yourself ` Falling` as you feel the abdomen let go, empty and relax.

If the mind wanders into thoughts of other things, don't worry! As soon as you realise this simply return to observing your breath noting 'Rising' as you inhale, and 'Falling' as you exhale.

This is all the practice consists of.

Breathing in – think 'rising' feeling the breath flow in.

Breathing out – think 'falling' feeling the breath flow out.

Simply continue in this way.

Avoid judging yourself in any way. In time your concentration will improve. Remember, the process of *remembering* to bring your focus back to *feeling* and *noting* the passage of your breath is a vital part of this practice.

"The process and the goal are not separate – they are one"

Mind-Brain Balancing Breaths

Pranayama 'alternate nostril breathing,' regulates the flow of oxygen and prana directly into the right and left hemispheres of the brain creating a sense of balance. This also relates to the balance of the chakras that are discussed in Your Spirit. This process automatically calms your central nervous system, clearing your mind of static and superficial internal dialogue.

When life gets too much and you just can't think clearly or feel confused this practice brings a sense of clarity and focus.

Right side of the Brain	Left side of the Brain
Dreams	Logic
Visualisation	Reason
Rhythm	Writing
Symbols	Reading
Recognition	Mathematics
Imagination	Language
Intuition	Analysis
Emotion	Factual
Subconscious	Conscious

In addition this alternate nostril breathing is a helpful antidote for clearing blocked sinuses, headaches, migraines and feelings of overwhelm.

Best practice sitting upright with a straight spine.

Traditionally men use their right hand and women their left hand to control the nasal passages. Using the right hand balances the left side of the brain which governs conceptual and analytical thinking, and the left hand balances the right brain which governs abstract and imaginative thought processes.

The Practice

Begin with a deep inhalation whilst lifting your hand to your nose.

Close the nearside nostril with your thumb, place your middle finger between the eyebrows, slightly pushing upwards.

Then exhale completely through the opposite, open nostril.

Now breathe into the abdomen through that open nostril and close it off with your middle finger.

Holding both nostrils closed with eyes shut retain the breath in your abdomen for 5 seconds. Roll your eyes inward and up. (eventually work up to 10 seconds)

Then release the opposite nostril and exhale completely and pause for a second.

Now breathe in through that open nostril into the abdomen and

close it off with your middle finger. Again both nostrils are closed.

Hold the breath for 5 seconds then release the opposite nostril and exhale.

Continue in this way for 6 rounds.

To complete this practice gently place your hands on your legs and be aware of both nostrils breathing freely.

Breathing during therapy sessions

The following exercises are to be used in the treatment room at various stages to help you empower and protect yourself.

In the chapter `Your Body` we discussed exercises that prevent you from `short circuiting`, helping you to draw on a more infinite and resourceful source of energy. All body care exercises are further enhanced by integrating breathing into them. The following are excellent for this purpose.

Earth Energy Re-cycle Breath

This exercise originates from the Chi Quong tradition which focuses on circulating and harnessing the energy of the breath within certain postures. A posture is essentially a physical configuration of a more subtle network of energy that generates a specific quality of being. The following exercise draws on utilising the infinite source of earth energy and circulating it around the body.

As you work around the couch you may become tired or lacking in the quality of energy you need to fulfil the treatment. This exercise will effortlessly fuel your movements from the physical to the subtle aspects of the treatment.

Imagine that as you breathe in, the breath flows in through the soles of your feet, up from the earth beneath you.

Feel the breath travel up your legs and spine, all the way to your shoulders.

Then as you exhale imagine the breath flows down your arms,

And into your hands, recharging them with vital earth energy.

Continue to re-cycle the breath in this way

Simply continue to work with your focus on the infinite source of energy coming in through your feet and out of your hands.

You will feel recharged in no time.

Initiating opening Breaths

Set the tone of the treatment by beginning each session with guiding your client to breathe. This serves as an opportunity for you to anchor into your own breath. It is a simple and straight-forward practice which allows both your breath and the clients to meet consciously, setting in motion a more receptive and energised space.

For yourself practice the `Fountain Breath` from the chapter Your Spirit to clear your space and then practice the `Earth Energy Re-cycling Breath' throughout the session.

Follow these guidelines when the client is lying on their front

Place one hand on their lower back and one hand between the

shoulders.

Let your touch be light yet relaxed.

When you feel their body rise on the inhale just let your hand be pushed up.

When you feel the exhale let your hand fall gently into their body, feeling connected.

When the client is on their back

Place one hand on the abdomen or solar plexus and one hand on the forehead, above the eyebrows.

Ask your client to breathe in saying

"Breath deeply all the way into your abdomen, then exhale completely. Just letting go into the couch. Breathe like this a few times"

During this time you can practice your own breaths.

Working Together

As a therapist you may well know different techniques for observing posture to see where there is an imbalance or be able to feel where tension is being held. There may be obvious physical signs such as raised shoulders, distorted hips, lower back stiffness, poor neck flexibility or crunchy connective tissue around the joints.

However, you may also sense less obvious areas of stress and tension that only become apparent when your client breathes into them. This is very telling indeed! These blocked or tense areas are often buried deep beneath the surface, in the soft tissue and corresponding nerves where the breath may not circulate thoroughly. These areas are often starved of oxygen and prana and therefore are out of touch with the clients' day- to- day level of consciousness and to the feelings hidden there.

Even though your touch may be quite light whilst working in these areas, you may still elicit a major reaction from your client as their response can be associated with more emotional issues, toxic waste, past trauma or deep tissue scars from old injuries.

You may have begun to work without the breath but when you

can see that the client is resisting your massage or other body work techniques by flinching, crying out or becoming even tenser, it is time to encourage them to breathe into it. By breathing into the tense or uncomfortable feelings you are helping them to let go and come through that process cushioned and supported by the circulation of oxygen, prana and awareness.

Encouraging your client to breathe

In the chapter Your Mind we discuss how it is the clients' *relationship* to their body, stress or pain that is often the most challenging aspect of the treatment that therapists work with whether you are aware of it or not. Breathing consciously can help you to work together to experience the best results.

The breath moves like a refined tool, a catalyst, that pushes through the habitual blocks and resistance that can be responsible for 50% or even more, of held tensions.

Your understanding of how breathing changes acid and alkaline levels, improves circulation, calms the mind and can take us to deeper levels of relaxation and awareness is powerful knowledge to serve your client effectively. Their participation in the process of letting go becomes an essential factor in the short and long term benefits of releasing pain or tension. It naturally follows that by encouraging your client to breathe you are reducing the amount of energy otherwise required by you. You are also empowering your client to bring their energy and consciousness into the equation, greatly enhancing their self-awareness.

Directing the clients breathing at specific times during a treatment adds unquantifiable value to the session, completely transforming the experience. The breath is the bridge between the body and the mind that can go beyond the obvious into a deeper awareness, or even spiritual consciousness, where insights and reconciliation arise.

This is not Cathartic

Please be aware that you are not in a position to create a cathartic experience or cause your client unnecessary suffering. You are only facilitating an opportunity to release acceptable levels of discomfort and tension within the framework of your therapeutic skills and techniques.

There may well be internal adjustments that arise within the client as a natural consequence of the breathing and body-work process. This is simply the organic re-alignment of the physical aspects of the body tuning into the more subtle emotional and psychological associations. The process of healing is now underway.

Breath as an instrument for Letting Go of Pain
This breath can be utilised whilst carrying out deep tissue techniques, accupressure or more subtle energy holds.

When you are working deeply in the connective tissue or soft fascia of the internal organs follow the directives below.

The Technique for Deep Work
Place your fingers or hold at the beginning of the stroke you are about to carry out and ask your client to *"Breathe into the touch."*

As you move your fingers more deeply into the tense tissue or muscle, through acupressure or petrisage, ask your client to *"Exhale out any tensions through the mouth."*

The principle here is that Inhaling into the beginning of the stroke brings energy, oxygen and consciousness to the blocked or congested area. Exhaling as the tensions are dissolved and dispersed allows excess carbons, stress and associated thoughts to be released through the breath.

Often the client will have a tendency to flinch and resist the release of tension which can re-enforce it. By helping them to breathe out tensions, the clients' level of release and relaxation are also increased.

The Technique for Light Work
This principle of breathing into a feeling or point of sensitivity and exhaling out any unwanted or painful feelings can also be applied

to more subtle energy holds. Just placing your hands on an area that is too sensitive for deep physical work and guiding your client to breathe in the same way is equally beneficial. Again it brings consciousness, circulation, prana, and oxygen to the area thatwhich are all refreshing and regenerating principles.

Follow the Healing and Integration Breath below for light body -work.

Healing and Integration Breath

When tensions have been released through deep tissue or connective tissue techniques the client will have experienced physical pain often accompanied by emotional release of tears or exhaustion. If the client has cried or is internally feeling vulnerable or just 'different' a moment of repose is the correct way to restore balance. In this new internal environment a re-adjustment is taking place that requires the purity of stillness and attention, rather than more movement.

After such integral work it is important to give your client time for integration and restoration. It is in this phase that insights and reconciliation can arise when the client has let go and is now floating in a new sphere of being that needs space. On a physical level this allows the skin and soft tissue to re-balance itself and promotes a more subtle circulation of prana and energy to act as a post release healing balm. On a more subtle level stillness acknowledges and honours the inner experience of the client allowing them to feel nurtured on a more emotional and psycho-physiological level.

In addition the skin itself may have been slightly disturbed, momentarily red from blood circulating to the surface. This is normal and a still hold will also bring a welcome pause to the process that has gone before.

This breath also serves as a release for you the therapist, so that you are not absorbing the released tension or negativity and gives you an opportunity to recharge and re-balance yourself. This practice is for both of you.

The Practice

Place your hands side by side gently on the area you have worked deeply.

Allow your hands to relax into the surface of their skin with full palm contact.

Ask your client to *'breathe as deeply as you need to into the area, and as you exhale relax into yourself'.'*

Keep contact with hands for 20 seconds whilst you practice Earth Re-cycling Breath for your own energy.

Before you take your hands away practice one Fountain Breath from Your Spirit to offer up any surplus energy.

CHAPTER THREE

KEY NUMBER THREE

YOUR MIND

What is this mind but a mirror of the trees that keep watch along the water.

Unknown author from zen tradition

The reality of your life and the actuality of your body reveal many things about you. Your mind is the map and your body is the territory telling the story of your life like a book, in subtle and more obvious ways. As it appears impossible to separate the body from the mind think of it as the body-mind. You may be in touch with the drama and dharma (purpose) of your life or not; conscious of how you feel or not, yet either way your body-mind tells a story that is uniquely you. Everything about you is signature and the tiniest detail in your estimation may be staggeringly obvious to others. The way you walk, talk, move, write, touch and smell are all powerful signature traits of your individuality.

The body-mind digests all of your conscious and unconscious experiences, thoughts, feelings, sensations and levels of waste matter on a cellular and psychic level, inevitably revealing the evidence of how you have lived. You are the sum total of all that you have lived through in body, mind and spirit. Your body is The Body of Evidence.

Karma

Our lives are experienced within the containment of this singular body, and we are often oblivious to the impact life has on us and how changes gradually occur over time. Whether these experiences are positive, uplifting ones, or negative in the form of trauma, tension or toxicity, these are the karmic vibrations that can become holding patterns which eventually define and shape us.

The body does not lie, its' physical strength and scars, emotional highs and lows, psychological insight and insecurities become lodged in our moment to moment reality and can control how energy is circulated from the more subtle feelings to powerful physical sensations and behaviour.

The very nature of hands-on therapy puts you directly in touch with the life of your client; their past *and* present experiences; in touch with their physical reality, their 'Karma.' Karma is the law of *cause and effect* meaning that everything has an outcome. The law of karma teaches us that nothing exists in isolation. That all things are *connected* and *co-dependent* to what has *caused* them in the past, and also to how they effect the present and future.

Karma is the unceasing re-cycling of energy in all its forms. The physical, emotional, mental, electrical, vibrational and spiritual. This philosophy or concept is based on the understanding that energy does not just disappear into air or space, (which in itself is also energy) but is naturally re-cycled and returns to its origin with the same energy with which it was created! It is a cyclic 'boomerang' affect. New energy is being generated all the time, but its sources have been here for a very, very long time. This is why in spiritual and religious doctrine the lineage is seen as so important. It is the line of energy that connects our faith or belief with those that had the same faith before, linking the mind and heart to an unbroken stream of consciousness .

Karma happens whether we 'intend' for it to or not! It is the unavoidable circulation of life experiences that characterise our individuality. The philosophy of karma originates from eastern spiritual traditions predominantly Buddhism and Vedanta. The basic premise for the belief in karma is that we are born many times and that each birth carries the lessons and energy of our past life, both good and bad, which in effect, *is* our karma. This philosophy also reveals that we have all been born so many times before that everyone we meet has at one time been our mother, father, lover, brother, sister, husband, wife or friend .... the possibilities go on and on. This is real food for thought!

Karma can be interpreted as the roll-over of our conscious and unconscious thoughts and actions, from moment to moment, which influence what happens in our lives. On a deeper level of the soul, understanding our karma, can give your life its meaning and purpose and therefore, direction. It shows you what aspects of your life require more awareness for inspiring positive change, health and happiness. When we look closely our karma shows us where we need to develop ourselves so that we can grow to our full potential.

Trans-form-ation and Habitual Holding Patterns
Through these cycles of life we generate patterns of posture, habitual thought and behaviour that become the unique character-istics and qualities of each one of us. Some of these habits become physical, emotional or psychological limitations preventing us from moving forward and often remain unconsciously held for years. They may manifest as negative thinking about yourself or others, poor posture or depression that can lead to further symptoms such as migraines, insomnia, poor digestion, consti-pation or even heart disease. The list is far too long! These habitual holding patterns can often be changed quite simply by just being aware of them as often as you can! Your awareness will create a counter-point that is observing and objective, consequently bringing the negative influence back into balance. Yet other patterns may be so deeply imbedded they require more structure and redirection to create the kind of changes needed to find total well-being.

Equally so, other habits can have empowering positive qualities that enrich our lives helping to regenerate more joy, health and creative thinking fulfilling our need for growth and transformation. The seeds for much of our thought processing are sown very early in our lives as children and it can be a worthwhile and interesting journey to reflect on how our conditioning, environments and parental care have influenced who we are.

We cannot *change* karma in relation to what has already happened but we can develop new ways of thinking in the present, that changes our relationship *to the past*. This creative positive attitude has a way of filtering down to the physical level, altering how the body feels, moves and expresses itself here and now, actually working to transform these habitual holding patterns.

This is why it is so important that we have a clear and conscious psychological understanding of the mental focus required to release stress and tension from the body itself.

You, the therapist, are the key to helping the client let go of their resistance and tensions, by bringing a positive and acceptant frame of mind to the space and to the treatment.

One Mind

The Equation of Thought

Thought create Words - Words create Meaning – Meaning create Feelings-Feelings creates life – Life creates Change – Change creates New Thought

Your thoughts are the seeds of the deed! As you think so shall you reap! All these well- known sayings are invested in a profound truth that is in operation every moment of our lives. The way you think about yourself also effects how others feel and think about you! We are mirrors to each other. Therefore you can use your thinking to create a positive, acceptance and healing energy as you work and in the process support the psychological well-being of your client. The state of your own mind is fundamental to the wholesome quality of a therapeutic treatment.

As we have seen everything and everyone is connected (even possibly related!) through the dynamic transference of energy from the mind and emotions.

When clients are deeply unaware of their state of mind, or are in a negative or karmic 'holding pattern', it can often make the therapists work a great deal harder. This is because you are working against a wall of resistance or unconsciousness on the deep level of the mind or emotion which in many instances controls the body. And, what resists persists! The best and most effective way of counter-balancing this is for you, the therapist, to be thinking positively, with your mind focused on your own centre, utilising all the other important keys set out in this book.

The Alchemy of your Mind

Psycho-neuro-immunology

The term *psycho-neuro-immunology* has been coined by American neuro-scientists who have recently made huge breakthroughs in identifying that there are actual chemical links between our psychology (the way we think), the nervous system and the endocrine glands, which govern our immunity.

Thinking positively is not only a psychological strategy for empowering your skills as a therapist, but research has shown that on a psycho-physiological level positive thoughts can and do alter our chemistry. This happens through the calming quality of positive thinking that sends relaxed signals to the hypothalamus at the brains stem. These signals then relay down through the central nervous system which in turn triggers the endocrine system to release hormones and neuro-chemicals directly into the blood stream. This process boosts the immune system and creates the physiological feelings of well-being which has similarities to the breaths journey that travels through the lungs to the limbic and circulatory system.

This evidence shows that negative, anxious or unhappy thoughts aggravate the nervous system causing the endocrine system to manufacture *acidic* neuro-chemicals that have a stress inducing effect. Over- acidity in the body and mind creates a hyper condition and can go on to cause impatience, aggression, headaches, allergies, skin problems, corrosion of the body tissue, poor digestion, excess gases, pressure on the veins and arteries which weaken the heart and inhibit circulation. It is a vicious circle.

On the other hand positive, calm inducing thoughts, create a more *alkaline* condition in the blood and therefore throughout the body and mind. This neutralises the effects of negative stress naturally creating a more balanced and healthy internal environment.

Consequently, it is in the interests of the therapist to make sure you are not adding unnecessary stress to your self or to the treatment by negative, judgemental or haphazard thinking. Discursive thinking can inhibit your energy levels and overall performance as a therapist and healer. Your own well-being will influence the clients experience and help them to release their anxiety more easily, preventing them from developing further acidity and stress.

Psychological Boundaries

If you are unaware of your own mind, the content of your thoughts and attitude you may be bringing your own tensions or distractions to the couch. Doing so makes you more susceptible to unwittingly absorb the tensions or negativity from your client. This is one of the common hazards facing the therapist. When unaware you are unprotected and without boundaries, open to absorb mental or emotional energy that is not yours, which can get lodged in your unconsciousness and filter down to a more physical level. This can then manifest in all kinds of disorienting and imbalance symptoms.

The combination of both client and therapist being in need of more consciousness will automatically dilute the potential benefits of the treatment either in the form of it being disturbing, non-effective, or ultimately draining the therapist.

Remember that you are in charge. That it is you who creates the environment for the treatment - and that also includes the psychological and emotional environment. Consciousness creates a boundary that protects you from potential hazards or negativity entering your sphere of operation.

Ask Yourself

What am I thinking? How do I feel? Am I at peace in myself? Do I feel present here and now? Am I easily distracted? Am I confident about my skills and techniques? Do I enjoy my work? If not, why not? Am I a positive thinking person? Do I feel compassion for my clients? Do I think I have enough training to achieve the required results? Do I feel balanced?

These are some of the questions that can show how you feel within and about yourself and what aspects need to be enhanced. Within this chapter you will find meditations and affirmations to help you along the path of self-awareness, making your work more harmonious and effective.

Making sure you have enough training and self-confidence is a primary requisite of developing your skills in all areas. The client will be able to feel your confidence, or lack of it, through your hands and perhaps in other ways too! If you work for your self make sure you keep up- to- date with techniques for further growth and if you are employed make sure that the treatments you are expected to give are well within your capabilities. All these points are discussed throughout this book and particularly in the key Your Space.

The following guidance and exercises will give you the tools to help you clear your mind, focus and develop more self-confidence.

Your Intent

Your intention, meaning the mental focus on the Purpose, Energy and Outcome you bring to your work is the spring-board from which the benefits of what you do will be experienced. Your intent is at the very heart of how your skills are met and are, in fact, an understatement to all that you think and do.

If you are presently going through difficulties in your personal life or at work this may dilute your energy and focus. At these times it is essential to use the power of your mind to re-enforce yourself with positive energy and *set your intention* bringing you back into balance. The recreation of your conscious intentions provide important energy boosts to your work at all times.

An intention does not necessarily have to be verbalised but words do empower your thoughts and speaking out loud or writing things down are extremely evocative. You can create affirmations of intent to repeat in your mind which also serve to set a precedence that can override any negative forces or influences in your environment.

Intention in action

Creating a positive and creative intent right at the beginning of your treatment helps to focus and protect your mind and heart throughout the session. Your initiating thought is the corner stone of your inner commitment to maintain stability and purpose and will carry you along with much less physical effort. This thought also helps to define the contours of your own mind, protecting it from negative impulses from wherever they may arise.

Be clear about the results you wish to achieve from your treatments and then it is simply a case of forming conscious thoughts around this goal and using words to create affirmations of intent. For example..

Affirmations of Intent for the Therapist
Example Opening Treatment Affirmations

"I intend to create a healing peaceful experience for my client (or name of)."

"I intend to help my client (or name of) through their pain to better health."

"I intend the best for my client (or name of) at all times."

"I am guided to give my best within the safety of my boundaries"

Ritualising the Intent

Your client will also benefit from being given the opportunity to consciously be part of the initiating intention. This is the purpose of Ritual and more information on rituals is in the chapter Your Spirit.

You can create a small ritual at the beginning of the session where you voice an intention for the outcome of the treatment. This can be done with incense, a smudge stick or sage to help your client re-focus and mentally prepare for the body- work ahead. This creates a powerful beginning that accesses the mind on the level of conscious thought and is therefore very influential.

Preparing the mind in this way is like setting the backdrop on the stage for a performance. The psychological environment has been painted with different colours, different words, altering the chemistry between the body and mind.

Affirmations as part of a Ritual
For example

"We intend for this session to bring an experience of harmony, balance and healing "

"We intend this session to clear the body and mind from any toxicity and feel free of tension"

Affirmations for Self Confidence
We can easily `leak` energy through negative thinking or allowing feelings of lack, or self reproach to get the better of us. So begin to transform your inner relationship with helpful, positive thoughts that protect you, adding valuable energy and depth to your work.

Create your own affirmations by using your own words and language to describe what is helpful and important to you. This process will also help you to become more aware of areas in your mind that need strengthening and therefore protecting. Say these affirmations quietly in the sanctity of your own mind.

Example affirmations for Self Confidence
"I am a clear and effective therapist."
Or
"I am confident in my ability to create the best possible treatment for my client"

Or
"I am a happy, warm person and a competent therapist."

Completing Cycles and Conscious Closure

How you complete a one- to- one session is as important as how you initiate it. Completing cycles is a dynamic technique that helps to disengage your mind thoroughly at the end of a session and serves to protect you from gaps in your awareness where you may drain energy. This also brings a conscious sense of closure to what has taken place, empowering the process, releasing you from one another. Your energy is retrieved and you complete with purpose. Conscious closure will help you feel lighter and re-energised for whatever you do next and seal the energy that has been positively exchanged. You can combine breathing techniques from the chapter Your Breath and spiritual guidance from the chapter Your Spirit along with these example affirmations or create your own.

Closing Treatment Affirmations

"I complete my work with ...(name of client) in peace and good energy".

"I wish ....(name of client) well in body, mind and spirit as I complete this session".

"May ...(client's name) enjoy the benefits of this treatment as I close the session"

"I close this exchange of energy completely freeing ...(client's name). and myself"

The Power of the Spoken Word

Language can be a great motivator, generating more confidence in the relationship you have with your client. By guiding your client with simple, supportive directives as you work with them, you can enable them to let go of stress and tension on a psychological as well as physical level. Words can create an empathy that soothes and satisfies the peripheral mind, softening any intense physical or emotional feelings and also to infer where energy should flow. When the direction of the mind is consciously engaged in the physical process it makes your work together easier and more effective.

In this way you are encouraging the client to liberate their *association* with their pain or stress. This creative process brings more *consciousness* to the treatment which in itself is *the* powerful transforming and healing element that facilitates real change. Through being verbally supportive and aware of the clients' internal experience you are speaking to their everyday cognitive mind. This generally helps to free up any fears or resistance of letting go that maybe unconsciously holding them back. Speaking gives them the spoken *permission* to release in the safety of your touch and awareness.

Embracing Resistance

However, hands-on, therapies of all disciplines can bring up intense feelings for the client. Their `inner radar` can sense the sensitivity of buried tensions and may be wary of the feelings that they intuitively know are waiting to rise to the surface to be released. This radar is also how the client protects their mind from engaging with any suppressed tension, so always work cautiously in the beginning until you feel they are really onboard with the process. What resists does persist and will further suppress the potential capacity to let go of old and toxic waste.

Through dialogue the client is being encouraged to go with and *accept* the tensions rather than resisting or ignoring them. By acknowledging tensions verbally, giving energy a voice, a connection is made that feels *safe* to let go because you are embracing their resistance in word and deed. In this way you can both achieve greater results and the client will experience a deeper sense of release and completion. Through the conscious process of accepting, of allowing the tense feelings to be felt, the association with the feeling changes. By reducing the resistance to feeling the stress or tension, the symptoms are also reduced.

Combining the breathing techniques given in Your Breath with directive dialogue, you can support the maximum release with the least pain and resistance. You will be guiding your client *to embrace their resistance,* achieving a deeper sense of relief.

Your client is then working with you, and not against you, making the demand on your energy so much lighter. They are going with the flow rather than against it. This process enriches the whole therapeutic experience often bringing to the surface a deeper awareness and insight into causes of imbalance.

Acceptance Creates a Space for Change

The psychology behind this approach rests in the belief that things only change when we can first of all accept them. This is a deeply contemplative way of thinking and is at the root of more spiritual principles of self-acceptance and forgiveness which are reflected further in the chapter Your Spirit.

Unacknowledged tensions may be pushed deeper into the body and mind generating more resistance.

Resistance *suppresses* that which we do not like or want, re-enforcing the condition, creating layers of tension. The opposite effect of what we really want! By accepting our feelings and sensations as they unfold, we are opening the pathways to a greater freedom of feeling and expression that is not bound by the restrictions of resistance. When we embrace resistance, we are on the one hand allowing the true sensation to be experienced connecting us with its source, and on the other hand we are reducing the pain of any unpleasant feelings by not claiming them or identifying with them. We let them go and thereby de-fuse them. By embracing the sensations as they arise we allow them to flow through us like a river, carrying with it any of the associated fears and tensions that dam the way to peace.

Research into the treatment of chronic physical pain, whether that be migraines, sciatica, arthritis, child-birth or other conditions, has shown that sufferers benefit greatly from relaxation therapy and meditations that are based on the principle of detaching from the pain by creating an observing attitude. Through exploring pain with a calm mind, breathing into the feelings, and in some techniques using visualization or internal dialogue, the association with the pain is transformed and the personal suffering subsides. We take a step back from the frontline and view our discomfort as if from a distance, objectively rather than subjectively. Compassionately rather than feeling as though you are a victim.

Encouraging an attitude of acceptance will automatically lighten your load as a therapist. You will be facilitating your client to let go on the level of self awareness, the level of the mind which is the prime mover. Acceptance creates a space for change.

The more resistance there is, the harder it can be to let go, so we use the `language of acceptance` to help change the clients' *relationship* to their tension. This is the psychological element of the process which is an important key to transformation. Releasing karmic holding patterns can cause emotional responses of laughter, tears or deep involuntary sounds of sensory relief as these blockages are felt, accepted and liberated.

As you work with your client you can feel the areas of resistance or imbalance in various ways. You may feel an intense heat coming from specific areas or restricted range of movement in the joints, or tight pockets of crystallized tension in the muscle tissue. Working deeply within these areas should not cause unacceptable pain; your role is to relax your client in body and mind through touch and raising their awareness of held tension, therefore their level of acceptance to letting go. This will naturally allow you to work more effectively without creating a `cathartic` experience!

What Not to Say
One very important point to keep in mind is that the client is doing this for themselves. Many times therapists will say " *Let go for me please*," Or "*Breathe in for me please*". This is NOT how to guide. Please do not tag *"for me"* onto your directive. They are not doing it for you, it is for them selves! The tone of your voice is also a key element in guiding your client peacefully. Find within you a gentle, compassionate voice that is caring and empathetic. A bossy, brisk tone of voice will not really do the trick!

As discussed in Your Breath use the clients' exhalation to apply releasing strokes, helping the body to clear and cleanse.

In addition to guiding the breath into areas of tension as you work, the following dialogue is also encouraging and supportive.

`Positive reinforcement acts like a natural tranquilizer`
J T Herron

Therapists Words of Support
Suggestions
"Let the couch support you, you can let go into the couch."

"Just let it go, you don't need that tension. You can let go and relax."

"Just bring your mind into the feeling. Embrace the feelings with your breath, then let them go"

"Allow your mind to be peaceful. Let go of any tension, relaxing into yourself"

Be Here Now Meditation
Hands on meditation to clear your mind
One of the best ways to create more self-awareness is to practice` Be Here Now`. This exercise puts you directly in touch with the moment, improving your focus and ability to maintain sensitivity and connection to your client, without being at the mercy of their condition. This practice contributes to forming your `boundaries` that protect you from unnecessary intrusion into the inner space and sanctuary of your own well-being.

The connection between your mind and your senses traverses a direct route, and by focusing on the pathways of sensory awareness which includes your hearing, touching, seeing, smelling and feeling can bring you unequivocally into the moment. These `doors of perception` are constantly picking up the changes in our reality and therefore keep us in touch with what is `real`, what is grounding, and leads us away from discursive thinking or emotional distractions.

You are the Key. By clearing and centring your own inner and outer space you can effectively facilitate the release of your clients' holding patterns. This then creates a pristine supportive environment for your work together.

Follow these guidelines as you carry out your body- work

Be aware of your feet *firmly* balanced beneath you.

Be aware of the *touch* of your hands on their body.

Put your *attention* into your *hands*.

Let your mind and hands *become one* experience.

If your mind wanders away from the present say to yourself
`I am here now,` bringing your cognitive mind into the moment.

Notice your breathing and focus on breathing deeply.

Feel the breath flowing in and out – saying inwardly ` *I am here now*`

Keep reminding yourself of where you are by tuning into your senses to bring you into the reality of the moment. Into Being Here Now.

Daily practice for the conscious therapist

Each day is new and brings with it the changes in your body and mind that growth and experience creates. Your cells are dying and regenerating themselves constantly and the process of re-connecting to your inner being is an on-going practice and discipline. This nurtures inspiration and awareness to all that you are and all that you do. We often expect ourselves to go on and on and not be affected by the passing days of hard work, the sharing of our lives with friends and family, and the natural progression of the years. Yet we need to remind ourselves of who we are and rediscover the true sense of the life within, on a regular basis.

One of the best ways of achieving this is in the still silence of simple meditation. Meditation can take many forms and there are techniques and disciplines from all traditions to learn and follow, some of which are in this book. The following practice is drawn from the Zen tradition and is a method by which you can empty and re-focus your mind, returning to zero, to begin again.

Zen Meditation develops a deep quietening of the peripheral mind, a process of listening to the voice within you. Your peripheral mind is the everyday chit-chat that goes on ceaselessly unless curtailed. This naturally attunes and re-connects you to your core centre that also protects your vital energy from leaking or acting unconsciously. Here, you are at the stillpoint of your mind generating an internal vibration of calm and equanimity.

This meditation is a profoundly simple practice perfect for harnessing the unwieldy antics of the mind. By using the functioning of the mind itself to focus, the practice combines your mental attention with the subtle sensation of breathing. You simply count your breaths from 1 to 10 and then begin again. This technique occupies the mind, synchronising counting with the actual feeling of the breath as it flows in and out. If you lose count, just return to one again beginning a fresh. This is called Zen mind – beginners mind, where we always have an opportunity to return to `one` and start again. Practice with a light - hearted attitude allowing your concentration to focus softly on your breath. You will feel calmer, brighter and more at one with yourself.

Practice each day for 15 to 30 minutes and you will be amazed at how the benefits build an inner scaffolding of centeredness, awareness and peace.

Sit in a quiet place and make sure you will be undisturbed.

Use a timer or alarm clock to set the length of your meditation so you are not checking the time.

The Practice
Close your eyes, sitting with a straight spine or can be practiced lying down.

Place your hands in your lap one upon the other.

Inwardly smile and relax your jaw.

Notice the breath flowing in through your nostrils to the abdomen.

One count is a whole inhale and exhalation.

Feel the breath flow **in and out** then - **count one**

Then feel the breath flow **in and out** – **count two**

And so on to **ten.**

If you lose count and the mind wanders, don`t worry

As soon as your remember

Just go back to one again.

Try not to berate or judge yourself. It is the process of remembering, of being able to bring yourself back to consciousness,

To remember your breath

This is the practice.

Simply continue in this way until your bell ends your meditation.

Sit for another moment and just be.

Rise slowly and have a great day…

Group Consciousness

Individual affirmation and meditations can undoubtedly alter the fabric of your personal well-being yet the spa as a whole will also benefit from the team working in this way together. As group meditation is such a sensitive and tender sharing of energy, focusing on the spiritual aspects of your collective well-being is a far safer, healing, and direct way of coming together to unite the consciousness of the team. The mind can be a fickle and self promoting force, and there are always those with more powerful egos or personalities than others. The heart centre is a more mutable, softer and forgiving part of our humanity and meditations that focus on spirit cultivate the heart chakra. The heart is the seat of the mind. In the following chapter, Your Spirit, we discuss the nurturing of the team spirit, the soul of the spa, and offer some practices, that automatically balance the mind and the psychological frame-work within which everything else takes place.

As we have read 'Intention' is at the very root of how energy evolves and manifests. The mind of the spa management is in control of understanding the importance of these more subtle, yet no less essential therapeutic principles. It is therefore the responsibility of those who organise the spa team, to make time for group work as a priority. As a conscious therapist you can suggest this to your managers for the total well-being of all involved, staff and clients alike.

CHAPTER FOUR

KEY NUMBER FOUR

YOUR SPIRIT

The Heart is the seat of the Mind

Bhudda

Opening the Door to Spirit

The purpose of turning this key is to awaken your connection with the universal source of energy of what some call spirit and others soul. To clarify these terms, I am interpreting the word spirit to mean a guiding energy that is not bound by the physical three- dimensional laws of the body or by the conditioning in the mind, yet nevertheless works through them. Spirit moves within you and around you in many forms, and some people can sense or see their own spirit guide, as another person or as 'energy', at times of healing or danger as a protective and benevolent presence. Spirit is the medium, the living channel for transferring energy for healing and clarity from one source to another. From one being or person to another.

Soul can be understood as the deepest inner form of your being, that journeys through this world at the very heart of who you are. Your soul is pure consciousness, always whole, profoundly sensitive and constantly evolving to fulfil the lessons of your karma in the turning world and perhaps beyond this too. Your soul retains the essence of who you really are, your true nature, no matter what, even though you may forget yourself and go astray.

Your soul is also your *conscience,* which speaks to you from the depths of your mind and heart reminding you of the omniscient qualities of love and belonging that are at your core. Your soul is connected to spirit by virtue of having a human body and defines your essence and individuality in the world.

The Healing Field of Energy

Your skin is a living breathing organ that not only functions as a physical barrier that separates you from other forms and holds all your organs in place, your skin is also highly sensitized by nerves to feel temperature, touch, vibration and electrical or energetic sensation. Around your skin is an electro-magnetic field of energy that is picking up information and translating it back to the brain-mind where your emotional and psychological responses originate. The reverse is also happening, as your internal feelings and thoughts influence this electro-magnetic field. Often we hear people say that someone has good or bad vibes! They are picking up on the sensory energy of that persons' aura and how it makes them feel. This is actually a spiritual connection.

You do not end at your skin, or begin there either! Your field of energy, your aura, is as much a living part of you as your stomach or feet. The body is electrical, has a multitude of vibrations and sensations that acts almost like a radar or a sheath around your body giving off and receiving energetic information.

From a spiritual perspective, illness or imbalance in the body or mind will affect the aura, your electro-magnetic field first, and then it filters down into the body as actual physical symptoms.

This subtle energy field is highly responsive and attuned to the dynamic of spiritual energy, because both vibrate at a very high frequency of movement. The physical body is relatively slow to react and respond compared to the lightening speed with which electrical and subtle spirit energy travels. The body is very dense in comparison and its particles large and heavy. The aura is diffuse, light, aesthetic and ethereal with particles that can be compared to light itself. This is why healing directly through the auric field can be so deeply felt and transformative. When the therapists' spiritual energy is in conscious touch with the clients' spiritual energy through the aura, healing and rebalancing can happen remarkably well.

The physics of this field have different dimensions and associations than our three dimensional world, which have been interpreted within many spiritual beliefs and healing practices. One of the most practical and applicable systems for the body therapist is working within the framework of the Seven Chakras as set out within this chapter.

There are many mediums that can help you as a therapist to work on a spiritual level with your client. Therefore, the contents of this chapter include ancient and well- proven philosophies, practices and meditations to feed and nourish our souls.

Acknowledging the Soul of Your Client

When a client comes for a spa treatment, which may be something as seemingly simple as a facial, or as complex as a watsu treatment, they are invariably there for something else too. On the very first page of this book we have seen how the spa has become a sacred space where people go to reconnect with their inner selves, their inner gods whoever they may be. The spa has become the house of the spirit that serves to bring us back home to ourselves in peace, tranquillity and serenity.

Clients are asking for an experience that brings more light, upliftment, energy, relaxation, harmony and beauty into their lives. People do want to be touched beneath the surface, to be reached and acknowledged on the deeper levels of their life experience. People do want to feel accepted and not judged, restored and inspired. In essence they want to be loved. We all want to be loved. They may not be able to voice this, and indeed do not need to, or they may be completely unaware of this impulse which is also perfect. The very nature of the spa empathises with this calling for inner peace, love and sanctuary and is the perfect environment in which to feel an abundance of good feelings flow through you. Love in itself is a force for healing.

The role of the therapist is to acknowledge this calling by

honouring your own spiritual energy and your own soul. To love your own soul, to love yourself. This is an unquantifiable and invaluable part of what you are offering and brings calming and caring vibrations to the session. You can only go as deep into another person as you can go into yourself. It is by healing your own wounds and scars and developing a compassionate sensitivity for yourself that you are able to tune in on an energetic and spiritual level to others. Your healing potential rests in the ability to empathise on a soul level with your client giving them a truly compassionate experience. Remember that you are the key that can help to unlock the doors of discomfort and disharmony, if only for a while, so that your client enters into the inner sanctuary and peace of their own heart and mind.

The Healing Crisis

The healing crisis acknowledges the process the body-mind can go through on its journey to balance and recovery. Sometimes we can feel worse before we feel better as toxicity and stress leave the system through all the channels available. Symptoms may manifest as colds, excess tiredness, diarrhoea, tearfulness, pimples, hyperacidity, headaches and physical pain. This is by no means always the case, but it is important to be aware of this tendency for the body to re-adjust itself. Deep massage, cleansing facials or body wraps may cause symptoms like this to arise. As the body releases the build-up of caffeine, alcohol, excess sugars, food preservatives, colon congestion, muscular and psychological tensions and other toxic waste, the real nature of these elements becomes more apparent. Assure your client by explaining as best you can about this process and encourage them to drink plenty of water, rest and exercise well.

In many circumstances repeating treatments three or four times will accelerate the release more efficiently, as one session may only touch the tip of the iceberg! The Healing Process is then completely underway.

Awakening The Team Spirit

A foolproof way of uniting the spirit of the spa would be for the whole team of therapists, management and reception staff to meditate together on a regular basis. The energy, intention and focus of the group as a whole is dynamically enriched by acknowledging together the underlying purpose of the spa environment. The team is only as good as the individuals who identify with the overall vision and intention. And the spa is only as good as the harmony of the team who work to fulfil its vision.

The important influence of each individual, their energetic and practical relationships, likes and dislikes, daily problems and conflicts can all become resolved within the purity of a group meditation. This cannot be underestimated. The impact the team has in maintaining the peace and quality of energy within the spa is key to its authenticity and success.

Sitting in peace together, with a structured meditation, even once a month, can transform the life in the spa, benefiting the most subtle aspects to the most pragmatic.

Cultivating Joy and Compassion

Holistic healing embraces the fundamental need of all beings to be held in an accepted and forgiving energy. Free from any judgment or analysis the body and mind are more likely to let go in a nurturing environment of loving kindness.

Your role as giver is to channel qualities of healing to create an internal environment within the client where peace is naturally restored. When peace is restored the innate self-healing powers of the individual come into play. Like attracts like. As we are all reflections of one another your first priority is to discover your own tranquillity and spiritual awareness.

We are all born with the potential, the capacity to be at peace yet somehow we have lost touch with and forgotten the intimacy of inner peace even though peace is a natural part of who you already are. We have accumulated an excess of impressions, sensations, experiences and conditioned responses that cloud the mind and heart and numb our greater sensitivity. Yet Peace is hidden there, waiting to be re-discovered and recognised. Peace is our own inner sanctuary and our first home. Peace is the true power of the human spirit that overcomes hardship and pain and has faith it is own nature. It is as much a means as it is an end.

We know what peace is not. It is not war, or strife, or greed or anger. Neither is it fear, jealousy or resentment. Peace does not exist in cruelty, in the fight for being right or the struggle for superiority. We need to call peace up within us into the fullness of our conscious awareness. Creating peace is making friends with ourselves and with our lives. We need to speak the language of peace so that we cultivate its presence in the reality of life.

Loving Kindness

The road to cultivating your peace begins with developing compassion for yourself and this path has been exquisitely formed into the practice of Metta Bhavana Meditation. Metta is a Pali word which means Loving Kindness, friendship or simply kindness and is an ancient Buddhist practice whose principles can be seen as the bedrock to many spiritual traditions and religious doctrines. If you have a religion or spiritual practice that you follow, this meditation will in no way deter you from it or clash with other doctrines. Metta is a pure practice that supports you, whatever your spiritual beliefs.

The joys of Metta reach us in ways you could not have imagined, as though you have drunk long and deep from the soul of life itself that softens and nurtures your innermost being. Metta is a balm for healing the human heart.

Meditation, in essence, is a state of fundamental rest.
Aitken Roshi, author of Zen Wave

The Four Main Principles of Metta Bhavana Meditation

Acceptance

The benefits of cultivating qualities of acceptance dissolves criticism, judgement, jealousy, loss, anger, emotional and physical pain, feelings of separation or isolation and create empathy, sympathy, deep relaxation and joy.

This principle of Acceptance is an important theme within body- work therapy as shown within this handbook. Acceptance becomes the therapists' invisible aid during therapy, which you bring to life through integrating the guidance given in the chapters Your Breath and Your Mind. Acceptance creates stillness and a space for change.

Gratitude

The benefits of cultivating feelings of gratitude dissolve craving, greed, grasping, frustration, selfishness and dissatisfaction and create qualities of appreciation, thankfulness, generosity and equanimity.

Unless you can appreciate your own body, your health, your sanity, your family, your friends, your abilities, your home and all the many riches within and around you, you will never be satisfied. By being thankful for who you are and what you have, more will be given in body, mind and spirit. Gratitude brings joy to the heart. Count your blessings.

Forgiveness

The benefits of generating qualities of forgiveness dissolve feelings of blame, guilt, sadness, grief, remorse and regret and create a powerful sense of inner freedom, healing, reconciliation and compassion.

Forgiveness can be a slow yet deeply healing process which does not mean that you condone whatever has occurred in the past. Neither does it mean that you forget any injustice that may have wounded you in any way. Forgiveness frees you from reliving the suffering caused by the continued feelings of grief or blame or regret in the present. Forgiveness is a force for reconciliation beyond the reasoning of the mind, allowing you to heal at the very heart of the matter.

The four most common hazards to peace and happiness

Regret - which causes us to hold on and live in the past.

Blame – which blocks true forgiveness.

Guilt – which is how we punish ourselves.

Anger – which is hidden or suppressed hurt.

Clearing the mind and heart of these elements makes space to plant new positive seeds that can grow into the quality of life that is your birthright.

Loving Kindness

The benefits of creating qualities of loving kindness dissolve feelings of struggle, strife, inadequacy and vulnerability, generating feelings of strength, protection, contentment, kindness and nurture.

In this world of diversity, where we can experience and witness the blessings of wealth, peace and wisdom, and the hardships of poverty, injustice, sickness and war a charitable mind and heart is a simple act of human kindness. Reflect on those that have been charitable to you and how you can be kind and generous also. Kindness is its own reward.

How far you go in life depends on your being tender with the young, compassionate with the aged, sympathetic with the striving, and tolerant of the weak and the strong. Because someday you will have been all of these.

George Washington Carver

Metta The Meditation Practice

Metta meditation practice is a simple process of sitting quietly and repeating specific phrases that relate to the above principles, slowly and silently within the sanctity of your own mind and heart. You can create your own language of Metta in the way that you think if you chose. Here Metta is presented in its traditional form which carries with it the blessings and energy of all those who have practiced in exactly this way since Bhudda gave us this great teaching 2000 years ago.

The practice can be focused on to extend out to other people in your life and throughout the world in a more global context. However, for the purpose of this book we are embracing the fundamental elements of metta which is to nurture and heal your self, the benefits of which will extend out to all whose lives you touch.

Begin with Breath Meditation

To enable you to focus as clearly as possible it is best to begin with a ten minute breathing meditation as described in the **Breath Awareness Meditation** in the chapter Your Breath.

Softly close your eyes.

Be aware of your inner posture, your breath and how you feel.

Practice repeating each of the qualities for 5-10 minutes, then flow to the next.

Allow your breath to help you relax into the beauty of this meditation.

Acceptance

Saying peacefully to your self

`As I am, may I completely accept myself`. I completely accept myself`

Allow qualities of acceptance to flow through you.

Relax into yourself, completely accepting how you feel

If resistant or contrary feelings arise, breathe into them

And accept them also.

Repeating slowly with each breath

`As I am I completely accept myself`. I completely accept myself`

Gratitude

Saying peacefully to yourself

'May I be thankful for all that has been given. May I be thankful`.

Bring to mind all that you are and all that you have.

Allow feelings of appreciation and thankfulness to flow through you.

If negative or contrary feelings arise, breathe into them, relax and let them go.

Repeating slowly in your mind

'May I be thankful for all that has been given. May I am thankful`.

Forgiveness of self

Saying peacefully to yourself

"May I forgive myself for any harm I have caused myself or any other being. May I be forgiven"`

As you peacefully repeat the phrase allow any feelings of guilt, regret or remorse to come to the surface of your mind and heart.

Let feelings of forgiveness come to you, letting go of stress and relaxing.

Receiving feelings of forgiveness.

Repeating slowly in your mind

"May I forgive myself for any harm I have caused myself or any other being. May I be forgiven"`

Forgiveness of others

Forgiveness of others can be much harder to practice but I offer this to you in the event you wish to go deeper into forgiveness which is one of the most extraordinarily powerful and transformative elements of self-healing. This first meditation for *forgiveness of others* deepens the healing and expansion of your heart chakra. However, if there is someone in particular that you wish to forgive The Seed of Light visualisation offered below will help you pathe the way from your heart to theirs.

The Practice

Saying peacefully to yourself

"May I forgive any being who has ever harmed me. May I forgive.`

Let qualities of forgiveness flow out of you, relaxing into your body and breath. If feelings of blame or anger arise, breathe into them, relaxing into yourself.

Repeating slowly in your mind and heart

"May I forgive any being who has ever harmed me. May I forgive.`

Forgiveness of a specific person
With Seed of Light Visualisation
This is to be practiced when forgiving a specific person whose name you may or may not know.

The Practice
Imagine that you plant a seed of light within your heart.

Bring to mind the person you wish to forgive, seeing them if you can in your minds eye.

From the seed of light within you build a bridge of light from your heart to theirs.

Plant a seed of light in their heart and practice the following Metta.

Saying peacefully to yourself

"May I forgive you for any harm you have caused me. May I forgive you.`

This may bring up intense feelings of resentment, fear or anger. Breathe into these feelings focusing on the bridge of light from the seed in your heart to theirs. Breathe into that bridge.

Repeat the words slowly in your mind and in your heart.

"May I forgive you for any harm you have caused me. May I forgive you.`

Loving Kindness
This is the sealing element of a Metta Bhavana practice session that brings qualities of kindness and joy towards yourself and others.

Saying peacefully
"May I be happy
May I be peaceful
May I be free from suffering
As I am, may all beings be free"

Metta in The Therapy Room
Engaging your mind quietly in the Loving Kindness practice at the beginning or completion of a one to one session is the final healing balm for your clients' spirit and soul.

A joyous and kind- hearted way to complete would be at the point your hands are together as you withdraw at the end of the session, at your heart centre.

Preserving your concentration, saying inwardly in your own mind, to your client, the metta of Loving Kindness.

"As I am
May you be happy
May you be peaceful
May you be free from suffering."

Chakra Awareness

Your electro-magnetic field is influenced by subtle energies in the form of vortexes of dynamic energy called chakras. We have many chakras strategically functioning at critical points throughout the physical body, located where there is a concentration of energy that creates an interface forming a certain shape or configuration. For example, the palm of the hand is a chakra, the sole of the foot is a chakra, your knee is a chakra. However, in the west we have adopted the eastern philosophy of the seven chakra system that directly connects to the vertebrae along the spinal column. This is the view that we will take, as the associated knowledge about these seven key chakras opens up a wealth of insight into the connection between the body, mind and soul, and therefore helps your work as a body therapist.

The word 'chakra' means a wheel or sphere, and each one of the seven are depicted differently within varying schools of thought, yet understood to function within dedicated principles. Traditionally each chakra is drawn as a symbolic flower with a specific number of petals, but we will keep a simple representation of them here in the form of a circle. In your mind you can imagine that these chakras, are like huge three dimensional spheres of rotating energy, a mass of tiny particles or vapor, (or a constellation of stars) moving outside, inside and through your body in their own orbit. They therefore can be sensed to the front of you, in the back and within the framework of your body. Part of it, yet somehow beyond it. Not dense matter that can be weighed or measured, but aggregates of dynamic energy, the precursor and destination of physical matter. They can be felt as heat or cold, as dense or light sensation; seen as colour, shadow or light, yet they are not controlled by these same external elements. If you have ever had a Kirlian Photograph which captures this field of energy on film, you will have a sense of this attempt to describe them.

The chakras function as resource centres, banks or stations, whereby you can gain access and control of the workings and operations of the subtle energy system. Like all stations they can be very busy, congested or malfunctioning to the point of a standstill due to lack of organisation and awareness of what is needed to help that station operate at an optimum level of efficiency, or wellness. When one station is out of sink it usually impacts on the whole flow of energy throughout the network. These centres are influenced by the impact of internal and external emotional, psychological and spiritual experience. If they become blocked, inflamed or weakened the delicate balance is disturbed and various symptoms can arise.

Some very sensitive and attuned people can feel or see chakras and work with these forces exclusively. However, the purpose of the information in this book is to help you cultivate an awareness of the chakras through your own meditations and develop a wise relationship with the knowledge so that you can embrace these energies as you work with your clients. Techniques of Energy Balancing and Crystal Healing are simple therapeutic ways to regenerate and restore balance within the chakras, as well as Meditation.

Chakras and Pranic Healing

Each of the seven chakras has a specific location in relation to your physical body as well as a colour and characteristic attributes. These seven correspond with your seven endocrine glands that are a vital part of your psychological and emotional well- being. On a more subtle level the chakras are associated with the yogic physi- ology of nadis, which are the subtle energy channels that flow throughout the body carrying prana, that was discussed in the chapter Your Breath. These key seven chakras are woven into the network of the three main nadis situated within and around the spine and act as pranic door ways, allowing for an integration of pranic healing. Pranic healing happens when circulation of the vital energy in the body and mind are harmonised and balanced. Yoga is, in fact, a form of pranic healing as can be other forms of body-mind movement that invoke an emotional and spiritual response or awareness.

The three key nadis are Ida on the left side of the spine, which is intertwined with Pingali on the right side. They represent respectively the flow of female and male energies including essential heat and cold from the first to the sixth chakras. The central nadi, Shushumna, flows through the very centre of the spinal column from the first to the crown chakra. Therefore, the breathing techniques as laid out in the chapter Your Breath are also powerfully effective in balancing the flow of prana through these channels to the chakras.

The Seven Chakras

The First Chakra
Muladhara Chakra– Literally means Root or Base
   Relates to the nerve centre the Sacral Plexus
   Corresponds to the endocrine sex glands. In men the testes and the production of testosterone. In women the ovaries and the production of oestrogen and progesterone.

   Colour - deep earthy blood red
   Attributes - hot, passionate, magnetic, practical, physically powerful and energetic.
   Element – Earth
   Sense – Smell
   Symbol - a four petal lotus.

   Attributes Balanced – grounded, empathetic, attractive, pragmatic, survivor, protective, dynamic.

Attributes Imbalanced – ungrounded, misdirected, physical weakness, cruel, sadistic, masochistic due to the inability to empathise.

It is located at the very root of the spine, the coccyx and fills the pelvic bowl governing the sacral plexus. Muladhara occupies the largest point of chakra energy and is very dispersed. Its influence travels down through the hips and legs to the soles of the feet and relates to our survival and sense of grounded in the world. The power of Muladhara sparks life up into the body, forming our connection and balance with the gravitational pull of the earth. In women this first chakra overlaps into the second chakra due to the creative energy required by the womb. Muladhara is raw creative energy that governs the ability to connect up on a pragmatic level with the instinct to survive, and can develop into a powerful force for achieving your goals.

Second Chakra
Svadisthana Chakra –Means Her or Ones Special abode
  Relates to the nerve centre Prostatic Plexus
  Corresponds with the endocrine adrenal glands and kidneys, which produce three major hormones, including adrenalin which balance male and female qualities and empower the body to respond effectively under stress.

  Colour – deep orange
  Attributes - warmth, compassion, spiritual power, nurture, empathy, energy, creativity.
  Element – Water
  Sense – Taste
  Symbol - a six petal lotus

  Attributes Balanced –nurturing, patient, creative, caring, friendly, kind, relaxed, magnanimous, fertile, sense of belonging.
  Attributes Imbalanced – angry, irritable, frustrated, unfriendly, infertile, isolated, fluid retaining.
  This second chakra is situated in the region of the hara, the

storehouse of energy. Svadithana is acnchored firmly in the sacral areas of the spine and spread to the 4th and 5th lower lumbar vertebrae which effects the sacral and prostatic nerve plexus. This chakra relates to our sexuality and is the densest of the spinal energy centres. Buried emotions and unconscious feelings relate to this centre. The health and balance of the chakra greatly influences the other vortexes as it is our centre of gravity. The connection between the 1st and 2nd chakra is more present in women than in men due to the womb being in this area. Generally this translates as the need for women to nurture as a way to survive, where their sexual drive is intrinsically connected to pro-creation.

The Third Chakra
Manipura – literally means Jeweled Lotus.

Relates to the nerve centre Solar Plexus

Corresponds to the endocrine pancreas gland which produces digestive enzymes and two hormones, insulin and glucagons which balance blood sugar levels.

Colour – bright yellow like the sun

Attributes – inspirational, motivational, vital energy, individuality, intelligence, presence, directional, leadership

Element – Fire

Sense – Sight

Symbol - a ten petal lotus.

Attributes Balanced – qualities of personal magnetism, discipline, belief in oneself, self-confidence, meets challenges, overcomes hardship, trusting, faithful.

Attributes Imbalanced –lack of confidence, unfaithful and mistrustful, vulnerable, insecure, self-deprecating, self critical, analytical.

Manipura resides in the region of the solar plexus at the mid-dorsal area of the spine. This chakra is often depicted as a radiant sun and symbolises the growth, magnetism and direction of ones own personal power and goals. It is sometimes referred to as The Christ Centre due to its uniting qualities of head and heart and will. The expression of a divine will through personal willpower. It demands courage, faith, discipline and conscious will. The third chakra has a powerful influence over the central nervous system and can greatly enhance the ability to endure and persevere through its unshakable faith and commitment.

The Fourth Chakra
Anahata – literally means Not Stuck, Unbeaten or Unbroken or United

Relates to the nerve centre Cardiac Plexus

Corresponds to the endocrine the Thymus which relates to the heart. It stimulates the production lymphoid tissue and lymphocites which are very important to the development of immune system. During puberty the balance of the thymus gland is very important to protect the growing body and protect it from disease.

Colour – Soft light Green and soft deep Pink.

Attributes – healing, regeneration , growth, human love in body and soul, spiritual love, gratitude, acceptance, forgiveness, giving and receiving

Element – Air

Sense – Touch

Symbol - a twelve petal lotus.

Attributes Balanced – a responsive rather than reactionary temperament, sensitivity, happy, laughter, nurturing, forgiving, accepting, thankful, loving, abundant feelings. Unconditional Love and an affinity with spiritual expression and philosophy.

Attributes Imbalanced – reactionary, tearful, unhappiness, easily offended, demanding, needy, sadness, feelings of abandonment, loss, guilt, blame and remorse.

Anahata relates to the heart chakra and the unity of all living things. This fourth chakra governs the heart muscle and is situated in the chest cavity at the upper dorsal region of the spine. It spreads between the shoulder blades at the back and energy from anahata flows down the arms and hands. This is why your hands are the greatest force for healing. In the purest sense anahata works towards developing compassion and a true sense of active belonging within the greater family of spiritual humanity. The two beams of colour that come through the heart represent the equal balance of spiritual and human love we need to be happy and content.

The Fifth Chakra
Vishudda – literally means Purified

Relates to the nerve centre Laryngeal Plexus and the Vagus Nerve

Corresponds to the endocrine Thyroid and Parathyroid glands. This centre of endocrine activity is vital to normal physical growth as it stimulates cell metabolism and increases blood sugar levels. It also nourishes the bones by stimulating the release of calcium through the intestines, where it is absorbed.

Colour – Lapiz Lazuli Blue

Attributes – self expression, inner voice, fluid communication, receptive, ability to listen and respond, honesty, supportive, protective.

Element – Ether

Sense – Hearing

Symbol - a sixteen petal lotus.

Attributes Balanced – protective, honest speech, clear self expression, connected to an inner calling, receptive, good listener, attuned,

Attributes Imbalanced – unsure of oneself, envy, jealousy, too loud, self opinionated, dismissive, lying, ego promoting.

Vishudda governs the throat and neck area. It connects to the spine at the cervical vertebrae in the neck. This is a very delicate area and relates to the communication and ability to receive and listen. Pure self expression and a strong sense of honesty and truth are represented here. Vishudda relates to your inner voice and your intuitive understanding. A developed or evolved fifth chakra often reveals clairaudient abilities and gifts. The blue colour represents the fluidity of communication like a deep flowing river.

The Sixth Chakra
Ajna which literally means Command.
   Relates the nerve centre – Frontal lobe of the Brain
   Corresponds to the endocrine Pituitary Gland which plays an important role as the executive to the Hypothalamus which send messages throughout the whole endocrine system. It has two lobes, the frontal lobe is in control of movement   It produces Noradrenelin and GH, growth hormone essential for maintaining a balanced integration and acceptance of our changing body and selves.
   Colour – Indigo or Purple
   Attributes – inner vision, balance of right and left sides of brain, memory, recall, cognitive thinking, intelligence, sensory assimilation, sense of self, strategy, survival, psychological orien-tation, spiritual insight, concentration, focus, projection, mind power, self awareness, consciousness.
   Element – Mind
   Sense – Awareness
   Symbol – a two petal lotus
   Attributes Balanced – good concentration,   balanced mind, healthy , insightful, inspired, perspectives, highly intelligent, powerful focus, clarity, intention, purpose, awareness, leadership.
   Attributes Imbalanced – domineering, overpowering intellect, boredom, dullness, depression, manipulative, purposefully misleading, bossy, dictatorial, unconscious intention and thoughts.
   Ajna is often referred to as the Third Eye due to the shape and qualities of the pituitary gland which sits in close proximity to the corresponding endocrine Pineal Gland and radiates forward to the centre of the forehead. The sixth chakra resides exactly half way between the right and left hemispheres of the brain and is directly influential of the electrical currents flowing through this area. It floods the bowl configuration of the skull and relates to our sense of sanity as well as intuitive knowledge and visionary abilities. Our sense of perception and clairvoyance is generated from this

centre and has a powerful connection with the first and second chakras, our survival and sexual energies connect here at the Ajna centre. Concentration on this chakra in meditation can lead to a form of Samadhi, a transcendent state of mind The seed of our lives are created within the mind and Ajna Chakra represents the power of the mind in relation to belief and manifestation. This is the centre from which affirmation and visualizations are best focused. Our psychic and clairvoyant abilities originate at the Ajna centre.

The Seventh Chakra
Sahasrara which literally means Thousand Petal Lotus

Relates to the crown of the head, fontanel.

Corresponds to the endocrine Pineal Gland. This is the Master Gland, which secretes Melatonin and influences the function of our biological clock and the circadian cycles of night and day. The hormone is concerned with pigmentation and changes in skin colour. The pineal also secretes enzymes that are proven to regulate psychological and behavioural processes in puberty and menopausal changes and has been measured as larger in women.

Colour - White

Attributes – regulates the healthy function of all endocrine glands, sustains the flow of life energy, connects to a super-consciousness, the subconscious mind, aesthetic awareness, spacial awareness, self consciousness.

Element – Space

Sense – Consciousness

Symbol - a thousand petal lotus

Attributes Balanced – wisdom, understanding, giver of guidance, freedom from fear, spiritual and universal consciousness, soul enriched, balance to all other chakras, good health and recovery, ability to let go and move on. Recognises truth. Faith in Life.

Attributes Imbalanced – Psychosis, mental imbalance, neurosis and disorientation, constant ill health, out of touch with reality, poor recovery, continued poor choices for oneself, uncon-

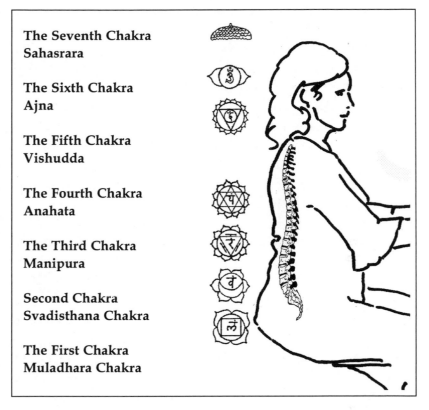

The Seventh Chakra
Sahasrara

The Sixth Chakra
Ajna

The Fifth Chakra
Vishudda

The Fourth Chakra
Anahata

The Third Chakra
Manipura

Second Chakra
Svadisthana Chakra

The First Chakra
Muladhara Chakra

sciousness, insanity.

The seventh chakra is situated on the crown of the head and is referred to as the Crown Chakra. It can be very large, enormous in fact, and radiates its light throughout the body and mind. Sahasrara relates to the flow of pure Life Energy entering the physical body at the opening on the crown. When this chakra closes down the physical body as we know it dies. At its highest level this chakra represents our divine consciousness and ability to connect with something bigger than ourselves, whether we call that god or not. An experience of Satori, of uninterrupted Samadhi, Divine Peace. This chakra contains all colours manifesting as pure white light symbolising the essential purity of life and of consciousness. It serves as an important doorway to a higher consciousness and is part of many yogic breathing and meditation techniques.

Energy Balancing Techniques in Treatment

Physical Symptoms and The Chakras

The information and knowledge of the chakra system is vast and you are encouraged to research the subject in more detail if you wish. In the descriptions that follow any physical symptoms of imbalance that may relate to the chakras has not been noted as there are so many possibilities. However, you are encouraged to think about the associations that an illness or imbalance may have based on the connection to nerves centres and areas of endocrine actvity.

For example, if constant migraines occur then Energy Balancing at the second and sixth chakras can serve to help circulate breath and calm the mind.

If there are panic attacks, heart disease or anxiety, balancing at the second and fourth chakra can serve to relax the heart and calm the solar plexus.

If there are problems with lower back pain or elimination then balancing the 1st and 2nd chakras can serve to bring energy to the area to increase circulation and calm nerve endings.

As you can see this is an intuitive and creative process which you will develop through your understanding and sensitivity over time.

Technique for Energising your Hands

An immediate technique to energise and feel the electro magnetism in your hands is to simply rub them vigorously together for about two minutes.

Then separate them a little feeling the heat and magnetism between them.

This practice also energises your hands before you begin body-work.

The methods that follow can be used on all the chakras for any physical, emotional or psychological imbalance to channel energy and spirit back into the frame.

Asking for Guidance- Receiving help

As part of your overall body- work session, creating a sense of stillness and tuning into the more subtle aspects of your client, supports healing and integration. You may already know which areas of your client need a more spiritual boost or balance or you may simply be drawn intuitively to certain centres. If you do not intuitively feel guided to any specific area you can ask for guidance. This simply opens up your higher mind, through the heart and crown chakras, allowing your everyday mind of choosing or not choosing, of reason and analysis, to be put aside. Opening yourself up to guidance and support from a source beyond the rational mind can be a great source of inspiration and healing whilst you work.

Simply say to yourself, *'Please guide me to heal and balance the energy of my client'*, or something like this. Use the Opening or Completion Chakra Balance techniques below at any time you feel the need for integration and stillness. Wherever you are working the techniques below can be applied to all energy balancing.

Opening Chakra Balance

This serves to balance and align the first root and seventh crown chakras, harmonising the positive and negative poles of the spine and connecting the energy up between them.

Place one hand on the 1st chakra at the base of the spine and the other on the Crown Chakra at the very top of the head.

Simply hold this area in stillness and peace, tuning into their breathing for a moment. Be aware of their breath also and guide them to breathe if you feel they need to relax more.

Then lift your hands away from the body a few inches in the electro-magnetic field, hovering as you maintain your concentration and awareness.

Continue with the treatment.

Completion Chakra Balance

This serves to integrate the clients' therapeutic experience and balances the letting go and regenerating process that occurs at the end of a session. The hara is the storehouse of energy and the forehead the ground for insight and planting new seeds of positive change and peace.

Place one hand at the 2nd Chakra on the abdomen just below the navel and the other at the 6th Chakra on the forehead,

Simply hold the energy here in stillness and conscious awareness of your own breath for a few moments.

Then slowly lift your hands away from the body and hover them a few inches in the electro-magnetic field above your client. Just allow yourself to feel whatever is there, breathing and accepting the energy.

Very slowly withdraw your hands completely leaving an energising presence in their place.

Bring your hands together in Prayer Mudra at the Heart Centre for completion.

A Journey through your Chakras
This visualisation meditation can be practiced either sitting or lying down with your eyes softly closed.

The benefits of this harmonious meditation will bring awareness and alignment to your seven chakras, creating a wonderful feeling of balance, strength and connection to your whole being. You may feel more open, bigger, brighter, lighter, happier and generally more at peace.

The artistry within this practice is to engage your imagination in the process of visualising the colour and thinking about the attributes of each chakra as you breathe into them. If you find it difficult to remember all the attributes, chose just one or two as suggested in the practice below. This may also trigger your memory and generate associated feelings. Repeat each breath cycle and visualisation into each chakra twice. Pause in between each chakra for a few reflective breaths.

The Meditation Practice

First Chakra – Grounding, Strengthening
Breathe all the way down to the base of your spine, holding the

breath there for five seconds.

As you are holding the breath imagine something deeply red like a crimson rose or red earth.

Bring the word *grounding* to mind

Then exhale down your legs, into your feet letting the red grounding energy flow downwards.

Second Chakra – Energising, Nourishing

Breathe all the way into your abdomen and hold the breath here for five seconds.

Whilst holding the breath imagine a deep orange colour, a fire or sunset glowing in your belly.

Bring the word *energising* to mind.

Then exhale down your legs to your feet filling up with glowing orange energy.

Third Chakra – Empowering, Confidence

Breathe into your solar plexus holding the breath for five seconds.

Whilst holding imagine a bright golden yellow colour like a radiant sun or molten gold glowing inside of you.

Bring the word *empowering* to mind

And exhale up your body, down your arms and out of your hands, letting golden light empower you.

Fourth Chakra – Healing, Loving

Breathe into your heart and chest holding the breath for five seconds.

Imagine soft green and pink swirls of light spiralled like a catharine wheel or a pink rose on a green stem. Brightening, awakening, softening and healing.

Bring the words *healing and loving* to mind

Then exhale healing loving energy down your arms into the palms of your hands.

Fifth Chakra – Communication, Inner Voice

Breathe as if into your throat holding the breath there for five seconds.

Imagine a deep river of blue flowing freely through your throat, relaxing and cooling it.

Bring to mind the word *communication* or *my inner voice.*

Then exhale as if out of your ears letting the blue cleanse them and free up your hearing and inner voice.

Sixth Chakra – Focus, Insight

Breathe as if up into the centre of your forehead, rolling your eyes inwards and upwards.

Imagine a deep indigo flame or eye there, or an amethyst crystal imbedded in the centre of your mind.

Bring to mind the word *focus or insight.*

Then exhale the breath across your forehead and above your head through the crown letting purple light flow outwards.

Seventh Chakra – Transcend, Expand

Breathe as if into the space above your head rolling the eyes inwards and up.

Imagine a vast sparkling multi-coloured white radiant orb of light above your head. Like a planet circling above you.

Bring to mind the words *transcend and expand.*

Exhale up into that orb of light letting the pure radiand white light flow down all around you.

Connecting the Chakras

This is an important part of the meditation as it links up the chakras with your breath.

Breathe into the heart chakra and hold the breath for 5 seconds.

Then exhale half of that breath,

Inhale again into the hara and hold for 5 seconds

Then exhale through the crown chakra letting the energy pour down around you.

Completion Polarity Breath

This practice is not necessarily done with the chakra meditation but can be practiced by itself as a wonderful balance for connecting to the forces of gravity beneath us and the forces of levity above. The magnetic energy and pull of the earth beneath you, keeps you grounded and centred, whereas the forces above you keep you upright with the potential for spiritual insight and experience. You are the bridge between density and light; between the finite and infinite.

Inhale deeply into the root chakra at the base of your spine
Hold the breath there for a five seconds
Imagining a root extends from the base of your spine
Down into the centre of the Earth
Then Exhale down that root
The breath flowing down beneath you.
Become aware of the pull of gravity
the magnetism, the density and stability holding you down.
Then, maintaining that awareness of your connection to the earth
Inhale into the heart and solar plexus filling the diaphragm
Holding the breath there for five seconds
Imagining there is a fountain of light flowing up into the crown chakra
Then Exhale up into that fountain
way above your head
into the spaciousness above and beyond you.
Letting the light shower down around you returning to the
the Earth.
Now just sit in that **Polarity**
In that awareness of the
stability beneath you
and the **spaciousness** above your head
Your breath flowing through you at the very centre of your being.
Be at peace, relaxing in the balance.

Creating a Sense of Ritual

Today many spas are offering rituals rather than treatments and we need to acknowledge exactly what the difference is between them. A ritual by nature includes the therapists own state of mind and participation, as well as the therapeutic techniques, communication skills, orchestration, organization, spirit and effectiveness of the products.

The manner in which a treatment ritual is carried out can instil a sense of ceremony; a continuity of awareness of its purpose and intention that embraces the well being of the whole person body, mind and soul. The Intention of a ritual needs to be communicated in such a way that the client feels involved and understands what is intended as part of the process. A ritual is designed to bring new perspectives so that your client, who may be receiving a de-tox ritual is not thinking about emails and doing the shopping. Through their senses of sight, smell, sound, touch, breath, focus and even taste they are transported to another space, another level of awareness where the processes of relaxation, de-toxification and re-balancing are experienced.

The beginning 'initiation' and ending 'completion' for each ritual requires a sense of purpose that can draw on the cultural heritage of the country of origin perhaps utilizing indigenous plants, flowers, herbs, sounds, colours and other signature characteristics of that culture. This will create a natural link to the environment, an important and powerful aspect of any authentic spa body therapy. Burning fresh herbs, meditation techniques, affirmations and breathing techniques can all contribute to creating a conscious transition from what has gone before to the present initiation of the ritual. The purpose of the initiation is to help re-focus the mind so that your client is given an opportunity to benefit wholeheartedly from the ritual. This guides the clients' thoughts and feelings in an elevated direction, away from the usual everyday concerns they may have. Rituals are also visually decorative presentations of indigenous products which generate a ritual that reflects the culture and relative habitat of the spa.

Combining Meditation and Visualisation for Balance and Protection

Visualisation for Protection
You can use this practice if you feel vulnerable in any way whether that is with a client whose energy you find difficult to work with, or if you feel you need extra support.

Imagine that you are surrounded by a sheath of white radiant light.

Let the light fall like a veil in front of your from your head to your feet.

To the back and both side of you in the same way

Let this light cover over the very crown of your head to a great height.

Visualise being surrounded by this white light whenever you wish.

Reflection
Throughout the chapters Your Mind, Your Breath and Your Spirit there are techniques for balancing, releasing, healing, opening and completing one to one sessions. All these practices are influenced and empowered by the integration and balance of your own conscious energy, your connection with the more spiritual and soulful aspects of yourself and hence others. Practicing the meditations in this chapter will develop your awareness and deeper sensibilities, mature your soul, giving unquantifiable quality to your healing potential and the overall energy with which you work. Your attunement will help you to empathise and experience that we are truly are not separate beings, we are united by virtue of having a soul.

CHAPTER FIVE

KEY NUMBER FIVE

YOUR SPACE

What comes from the depths
Enters the depths
When water is still the reflection is clear
The mind is the surface of the heart
The heart is the depth of the mind.

Bhudda

Spas and places of spectacular healing and beauty have been on this earth since time began. There have always been those who have sought out these places of tranquillity and inspiration that soothe our weary bodies and free our minds. The motivation behind the pilgrimage to these sanctuaries has not changed, the journey to the spa is still driven by a deep genetic yearning to return to the elements as the perfect environment to touch the source of ourselves. A space to be supported in body, mind and soul, liberated from the structure and interference of day- to- day life and know a seamless timelessness. A place to simply be, feeling the beauty, miracle and joy of this fleeting world.

Healing Waters

Water is the key element in our biological make-up, life having evolved from it, retaining an affinity and need for its nature.

A spa setting provides the space where the primary energy of water in all its varying temperatures and forms can be entered into, seen and heard. Whether that is in the form of water features, trickling springs, imaginative hydro pools, hot tubs and cold plunges or aromatic steam rooms, herbal baths, floatation pools and drench showers, water is the medium that transforms the space, cleansing and relaxing our body and mind.

The natural mineral spring spa has the added power of the geo-thermal hot water rich in magnesium sulphate (epsom salts), potassium, calcium, boron, silicon and many other trace elements. These elements seep through the skins' surface, into the muscles, viscera and bones, relieving pain and stress as well as offering a soporific quality that deeply relaxes body and mind. Pure Glacial Mountain Water and Dead Sea Salt Water also have their own distinct healing and life giving properties and continue to be a source of regeneration in many ways.

Water still remains the fundamental giver of life and has retained its mystical power of transformation, by its inherent purity, that defies mans' efforts to synthesise it in any form. Water can go far beyond manpower into the vaster realms where science meets spirit, nature meets man and beginnings meet endings. The various compositions and 'bodies of water' have the energy to create life and heal, or damage and end life, by its overwhelming weight and force.

The growth in drinking bottled mineral waters, from the celebrity favourite of pure Fiji Water to Evian or Buxton Spring Water has developed an industry that brings in £2 million a day! Water in all its forms is a magnetic and purifying substance that continues to envelop and mesmerise us, and will perhaps, some day, overwhelm most of our earth if the temperature of our planet continues to rise.

What is a spa?

The phenomenal growth in the industry has not only raised standards, expectations and performance, it has also given rise to a freedom of expression within the use of the name 'spa'. This can be confusing and misleading so we will take a look at the variety of situations and locations embracing this term.

The word 'spa' itself comes from the town of Spa in Belguim where the first recognized benefits of drinking the town's' natural iron bearing spring water for iron deficient illness was recognised in medieval times. However, the Roman idea of bathing in mineral waters for relaxation, re-creation and healing became symbolic of their cultural legacy and the 16th century saw a revival of spa towns when a certain, William Slingsly returned from Spa in Belgium and discovered an iron rich spring which became known as Harrogate, The English Spaw. Drinking the water rather than bathing in it, was the important part of the experience but as our knowledge of the therapeutic benefits of the water evolved, bathing became the main purpose of going to a Spa. Further research into the term spa, shows that the Walloon word for 'fountain' is 'espa', which has associations with the Latin word 'spagere' which means to moisten or sprinkle.

Essentially the term spa is now associated with therapies that include water as the key element, and is therefore used within a vast range of facilities and locations.

State- of- the- Art man- made spas are generally great guzzlers of our planetary resources and therefore not so eco-friendly to our environment. Consequently there is an innovative interest in new spa developments trying to re-design how to generate reusable sources of heat to fuel the environment. Spas that can draw on their natural resources, like the Mineral Hot springs, for instance. Thalassotherapy and Retreat Spas have an advantage in this respect. However, this issue is a growing universal concern and we will see a return to the more simple approach of how to address the needs of our well-being.

Mineral Hot Springs are locations that offer direct bathing in the natural hot spring water as it flows out of the earth. There are many of these powerful places of healing and regeneration around the world and whole towns or small communities have been built around them. In England, Bath has since Roman times, and perhaps before that, been a mecca for healing, and the hot spring culture is prevalent in Japan, America, Bulgaria, Hungary, Belgium, Scandinavia and many other remote regions. These places are often in beautiful, rolling or mountainous regions where there is extraordinary abundance of growth such as the Napa Valley in California, or unusual desert locations where the energy within the earth, colours and contours the landscape in interesting and inspirational forms. The geo-thermal hot water that is rich in minerals and trace elements brings a fundamental organic quality to the environment altering the aroma, water texture and therapeutic experience.

Many of the original natural mineral springs were places for ceremony and prayer where bathing was part of the spiritual purification ritual. As understanding the composition of spring water itself grew, these places became associated with medicinal therapeutic treatments for arthritis, rheumatic pain, muscular tension, depression, skin imbalance, respiratory disorders, nerve problems, convalescence, deep relaxation and longevity. In the surge of interest during the last ten years some of these places are offering a more eclectic approach to health, beauty and wellbeing. Upgrading their facilities for accommodation and treatments has put the more rustic and medicinal environment on the destination spa circuit. However, there still remain a number of totally pure, ethnic mineral hot springs such as Harbin and Orrs Hot Springs in California that have managed to retain the purity of offering the spirit of the water in its natural habitat. Hot springs may also have their own source of indigenous mineral rich mud and clays to use therapeutically. As places for educational experience and personal development it is highly recommend you take a course, work or stay for awhile in one of these sanctuaries of the water spirit.

Retreat Spas are a growing culture within themselves that draw their offerings for total well-being from their location, landscape and how the space is utilised for rituals, relaxation, treatments, activities and classes. Retreat spas may combine ayurvedic therapies with yoga, shamanism, dance therapies, deep meditation, sweat lodges made in tepees or yurts, rain-water plunge pools, mountain stream cleansing and wood-burning stove saunas and baths. The emphasis is on 'real retreat' that powerfully help to de-tox the body, mind and soul within a pure culture that includes the trees, earth and sky into the conscious experience of changing from the fast lane, to the mountain pass.

Thalassotherapy Spas are situated on or near the sea where thalassotherapy draws its identity and healing powers. The ocean is a rich source of minerals, salts and iodine, when combined with the sun creates a natural therapeutic spa experience. The benefits reach deeply into the blood stream as the salts cause the skin to expand and receive the beneficial 'oligoelements' inherent within the sea water. Seaweeds are also an effective source of antibiotic, antibacterial and antiviral properties. These spas utilise sea water in various temperatures in pools, baths and showers for therapeutic exercise, de-toxification, weight-loss, skin problems, inflammatory disorders, stress release, rejuvenation and revival. Locations all over the world, in Italy, France, Africa, Ireland, America, Greece, Malta, and more, now offer a modern fusion of body and beauty treatments that fulfil many of the demands of the discerning spa traveller.

Of course, a clean sea and sandy beach are the optimum thalassotherapy, and places where there is an abundance of salts and minerals such as the Dead Sea become important sources for therapeutic product ingredients and experience. Thalassotherapy is an invigorating and intensive, well worth discovering from a receiving and giving perspective.

Destination Spas today can be mini-universes within themselves providing the dedicated seeker of well-being everything to support them in living a healthy and holistic lifestyle. Destination Spas are becoming the optimum holiday for many who's need to de-tox, relax, re-charge and rejuvenate must re-dress the intensity with which they live their lives. As stress levels rise often due to technological pollution, our senses are bombarded through every channel, requiring refreshing new ways of taking a break that does include excessive eating, drinking or other forms of indulgence that adds further stress and toxicity. We are far more educated than we were 20 years ago about nutrition, exercise, stress levels, environmental hazards and regeneration and the media keeps us up to date with every new discovery regarding our health and well-being. The Destination Spa aims to fulfil this aspirational community with comprehensive treatment menus to include everything from holistic massage and facials, to rasuls, de-tox rituals, steam rooms, saunas, all forms of hydro-therapy, watsu, shiatsu, reflexology, aromatherapay, yoga, physical fitness, personal life coaching, nutritious food and special educational programs. However, too much choice or repetition of types of treatments can be confusing and stressful for the guest so a refined, well laid out and clear approach to the menu makes for easier bookings.

Often large areas devoted to separate male and female cleansing, steam, sauna, relaxation and changing areas also adds another bonus for those that like the freedom of single sex environ-ments, which more often are women rather than men! However, in equal measure, suites for couples to be bathe, be treated and relax together in total privacy are a wonderful intimate oppor-tunity to share real quality time which is so often spent apart in other spa settings.

Destination spas are geared towards creating a fluid client journey, integrating the spa philosophy into the hotel bedrooms, offering spa inspired turn-downs, bathroom products, music and an in-room consultation and therapy service which can create a whole new level of privacy and relaxation. These spas often offer personal de-tox or well-being retreats for the individual and are totally focused on making sure their personal service exceeds expectations by keeping up to date with new treatments and products. With the fusion in eastern and western cultural body and beauty therapies such as ayurveda and hammam; the interest and benefits of yoga and meditation; plus the ability to travel the globe easily and cheaply the immense variety of destination type spas is staggering. In these environments people feel free to wear robes in most areas, and move around as if they were at home, which is testament to the levels of relaxation achievable in a well thought through, destination spa. Though some destination spas may seem slightly more hedonistic than others, there appears to be a rising spiritual consciousness filtering through into the mainstream awareness influencing how we experience beauty, enjoy ourselves and share time together.

Day Spas offer a broad choice of body, mind and beauty therapies, without any residential accommodation. Within this category I also include the High Street and Urban Spa many of which now offer very similar services on a smaller scale. The philosophy and orientation of these spas can vary enormously depending on the product range, as this often dictates the quality of the overall experience. The day spa, like the destination spa, is a growing trend for the same reasons, and locations where large swimming pools, hydro-therapies, yoga, nutritional food and enjoyable relaxation areas are offered make an excellent mini-retreat or shared day out.

The Urban and High Street Day spa may not have adequate relaxation areas for post treatment integration, yet do provide a different kind of 'social' relaxation where waiting areas become resourceful and educational meeting places with books, leaflets and magazines about health and wellbeing to inspire and relax the mind. These places serve to raise awareness of how to best take care of yourself and those that may just come in for a waxing may suddenly decide to experience a de-toxifying body wrap! Innovative urban day spas use uplifting aromas all day and may have space for water features, testing of products and even hand and foot treatments whilst you chat to your friends. Working women will utilise these city escapes for distressing with an Indian head massage during lunch hour, aromatherapy or body wrap on the way home from work. For young mothers and the health conscious woman these spas offer a haven of reward and ultimate pampering to ease the harder edge of life.

The combination of elements offered now are far more inventive and unique than at any other time where perhaps a night club setting may offer spa facilities too! Day spas are embracing holistic health with colon cleansing, acupuncture and life coaching. There really seems to be no one formula for these very accessible sanctuaries.

For men, whole new venues dedicated to male grooming, that usually include hairdressing, wet-shaves, facials and massage are also flourishing with complete skin-care lines and treatment options being designed for them.

As a therapist, much can be enjoyed and learnt from these environments, the team spirit playing an important part of your day. Issues regarding dedicated room care, set-up, laundry, sales, relaxation areas, hygiene and protocols can make or break a day spa.

Medi-Spas have risen out of the growth in medical 'cosmetic procedure' that require licensed professionals to carry out more intensive transformative body and beauty treatments, within a supportive spa therapy service. The increase in devastating results for clients who have not had a professional service has raised awareness of the need for more strident monitoring of this area of beauty therapy.

The benefit of holistic and complimentary therapies easing the vibrational energy and healing of more medical and aesthetic treatments creates a more integrated caring service of well-being.

As a therapist you will need to have or cultivate an affinity with the specific work carried out in these spas, as contra-indications and limitations on how you work will need to be re-assessed.

Club Spas focus primarily on an environment to accommodate fitness, with probably a pool, gym and exercise classes of all kinds. Full membership drives these clubs which are often very busy places, as they tend to be more competitive and based on activity rather than relaxation. However, alongside these activities club spas do provide treatments and services to support total well-being. The treatment facilities will vary enormously from one club to the next, again depending on the overall philosophy, products, and location.

As a therapist, if you are particularly interested in Sports Massage, Deep Tissue massage or floor treatments such as Shiatsu or Thai Yoga Massage these can be educational and exciting places to work.

Hotel Spas who before may have had a small offering to guests, are now investing heavily in upgrading and training their spas to compete with this growth in demand. Expectations from guests visiting four and five star hotels have risen with the need for finding new ways to de-stress and enjoy hotel facilities. Usually the hotel spa is an added bonus to the hotel experience, where a pool, gym, sauna, steam and hydropool, also offering professional body and beauty treatments to help relax the weary traveller. They may also provide a healthy option food menu and hair salon service.

Working in a hotel spa can be a balancing act, especially if the hotel runs the spa itself, due to emphasis on the 'hotelery' culture being the predominant concern. Therefore, a hotel spa that has an independent management can often work better for those employed and guests alike, as recruitment, training and standards become more important issues. However, where a hotel has a passion for excellent leisure facilities as in the increase of six and seven star hotels, and an eye for what is happening in the spa industry they can be superb spas and innovative places to work.

Cruise Ship Spas are also taking on board the lavish and all-inclusive approach to offering deeply therapeutic environments, classes, rituals and treatments that support the total well-being of guests within a holiday setting. Huge investments in spa facilities on cruises have brought a need for well-trained, committed and team spirited therapists of all disciplines. Recruitment is quite rigorous as therapists work long hours, are out at sea and living within a very special community at close quarters. Employees will be required to carry out up to six weeks of training before going on board a cruise ship. For those that like to work intensively, are happy at sea, have fantastic fun and adventure, this is a unique working experience.

Spa Spaces

Hammam
The Hammam originates from Morocco whichand has entered our

culture through the popularity of the Turkish Bath tradition. The word is derived from the Moroccan word hmm which means 'heat' and hammams are the cultural 'bath house' where men and women can go to cleanse, relax and socialise in most Moroccan towns. Traditionally they consist of three interconnecting rooms, one warm where people wash themselves and each other; one very hot for steaming, and one cool to complete and balance the warmer rooms. Hammam are architecturally stunning buildings providing charismatic sanctuaries with domed stained glass ceilings, moorish alcoves, pillars, lanterns, tiling, marbling and hidden seating creating an inspiring use of light and space. The ritual requires people to wrap silk or cotton around themselves and take with them body brushes, hammam clay soap, jugs of water to wash and rinse themselves. Rigorous and energetic massage is sometimes available by professional masseurs, so not for the feint hearted or injured! A marble slab in a central area offers body scrubs and spa attendants cleansing rituals. Here, water is treated with great respect as it is not thought well to use too much as it is always in short supply in and highly valued. Men and women hammam separately where there are delicate etiquettes and traditions, though now private hammam are very common due to the interest from tourists in those countries of origin. The temperature of a hammam will probably not exceed about 40 degrees centigrade as the humidity in the atmosphere would scaold the skin.

Rasul

Rasuls have become the mini-hamman of the spa culture and can be tailored to fit into an urban setting as easily as in a five star spa. The word comes from the 'rasul mud' that is applied during these rituals. Rasuls accommodating from one to six people are designed to allow for individuals or groups to have a self-administered therapeutic treatment that combines a possible pre body scrub, then an application of body mud, face clay and after completing, applying hydrating body oils. The seats of a rasul are often heated from within 'draconian seats' where guests sit in the tiled dry heat chamber for about 20 minutes drying the mud to draw out impurities. Steam is then piped into the rasul which dissolves the mud, followed by a rain-like shower that washes the mud away. Some rasuls omit this last stage and simply use the shower for the final cleanse, which is integrated into the rasul suite. The quality of the products used and the balance of temperatures are essential to ensure an enjoyable experience. Rasuls do provide a worthwhile good quality treatment that can be a great financial asset to any spa. They are fun, can be shared with others and do not require therapist's time or skills.

Steam Rooms

Steaming is how we open the pores of the skin, increasing cell renewal, stimulating the sweat glands and lymphatic system to cleanse. The temperature, like the hammam, probably will not exceed 40 degrees as the skin could burn and it would be impossible to breathe in the ferocious wet heat. Steam rooms are more popular on the whole than the sauna as the heat is more superficial yet actually serves a different purpose. Using aromatic oils to breathe in the steam itself such as lemon, eucalyptus, lemongrass or lavender can further enhance the steaming process. Cool showers on completion are also highly effective as they close the pores of the skin, re-balance the internal body temperature, protecting it from any vulnerability when exposure to a chilly outside temperature or environmental pollution through the skins pores can prevail. Traditionally a steam should always come before a sauna so that the skin has been purified to receive the deeper heat.

Steaming is an excellent pre-treatment ritual before a scrub and body-wrap as the blood and lymph are brought powerfully to the surface enhancing the overall de-tox process, releasing excess fluids, supporting weight loss and skin cell renewal therapy.

Saunas

The sauna originates from Finland and the Finnish Sauna is also an ancient social custom which whole families share during the long winter months, rolling in the snow to cool down, gently beating each other with birch branches to improve the circulation and drinking beers afterwards to re-hydrate. Scandinavians believe that a good sauna can cure anything and some say a woman is most beautiful after a long sauna. The interior of this popular type of sauna is traditionally made of cedar, hemp or aspen wood, but redwood and combinations of wood can also be used, beech being a common choice for the actual benches.

Other cultures too have their own version of sauna/steam environments such as the Mexican Tamazcal, and the American Indian ceremonious rituals of Sweat Lodges that are still very popular today. Temperatures, due to the evaporation of moisture on the hot coals, rocks or stones can reach as high as 110 degrees without burning the skin due to the circulation of air through a vent, and the porous wood or canvas structure itself. A small bucket of water with ladle is kept inside to dowse the coals, instantly increasing the temperature by creating a steam evapo-ration. Sitting at the highest level within the sauna is hotter and lying down if you can is certainly more relaxing. Electric and infrared stoves are most commonly used in Finnish Style saunas, though the traditional wood burning stove is a truly wonderful experience. The intense dry heat reaches deep within the muscles and joints, pushing out the toxins hidden there. Saunas are excellent for respiratory, arthritic and rheumatic problems improving circulation, and burning sandalwood, eucalyptus or sage within a sauna is very therapeutic. Massaging therapeutic oils into the skin whilst in the sauna draws the ingredients into the muscles with great efficiency. Peoples tolerance levels of the heat varis but a recommended 10 -20 minutes is sufficient.

The heat draws the blood to the surface creating strong perspi-ration and therefore a cold plunge or cold shower after each sauna is essential to re-balance the circulation, close the pores of the skin and tone the muscles back up, so they are not left warm and vulnerable. Cold water also helps the de-tox process and two or three rounds of sauna and cold water generate a tremendous boost to the circulation and immune system protecting you from ill health. If there is some snow right outside take a roll in it instead or use the wonderful 'Ice Rooms' slowly coming into the spa space.

Saunas are an excellent pre-massage ritual as they deeply relax the muscles and joints improving the process of letting go and re-balancing. Those with high or low blood pressure will need to be careful carrying out the hot and cold frequency as it may be too much stimulation for the heart.

Ice Rooms
Ice rooms are a total luxury, unless you are in the North Pole, where the environment can sustain the icy temperatures otherwise generated through refrigerating systems. As the perfect anti-dote to the heat of steam and sauna, ice rooms intensify the boost to your circulation, toning the skin and creating a wonderful thera-peutic balance reducing inflammation, skin degeneration and stimulates skin cell renewal important as an 'age defying' aid. Ice troughs outside steam and saunas to rub into your face and other area of your body are an alternative approach.

Cold Plunge Pool
A cold plunge pool can be as simple as a cold tub of water that is big enough for one person to completely submerge their whole body, including dunking their head in one fell swoop. This instantly contracts the muscles, balancing the expanding effects of any deep heat treatment. Powerfully stimulating and refreshing the blood rushes to the extremities, including the head and heart, and is the ultimate 'internal dialogue stopper'! Not for those with high or low blood pressure or a weak heart, it is however, a wonderful feel-good boost for your circulation, brain cells, mind and emotions as the endocrine system is prompted to manufacture your 'own inner pharmacy' of stress relieving neuro-chemicals and hormones recharging and re-patterning your psycho- physio-logical responses. The sauna and plunge pool, or some form of immediate 'dunking', together create the perfect 'psycho-neuro-immunology' therapy session. Simple and self- administered, combining the best body mind shake-up and shake down.

Aroma Rooms

Awakening the senses, particularly our sense of smell, creates an avenue through which the mind and emotions can be deeply relaxed and transported. Aroma rooms draw on the power of calming and uplifting essential oils within a contained environment that is atmospherically cool, with tiled benches or loungers that are heated from within. The spas choice of essential oils can be tricky as peoples preferences vary greatly. Only 100% pure essential oils will do. A light, either citrus based or a combination of woody and floral aromas that are easily inhaled will not overwhelm guests, and the cool room creates a relaxing alternative to the hotter spaces.

Wet Rooms

The wet room provides the space to carry out treatments where water is a key part of the therapy, freely flowing from some aperture or shower over the coach and client onto the floor. Alternatively, the wet room may simply accommodate the easy procedure for a body scrub or wrap where a large shower area is in the room itself. The design of these rooms will usually see slightly tilting floors towards a major drain that is large enough to drain away muds, salts, seaweeds and clays that may be used within the treatment. Wet rooms are wonderful places to receive treatments, though quite an art for the therapist whose aim to keep dry and presentable throughout requires innovative room layout and practical clothing design.

Kraxen Stove

The Kraxen stove uses therapeutic Alpine Hay which is steam heated within specially designed warm chambers to release their therapeutic benefits. The chamber is created as a shared space with individual alcoves where you sit in a light robe with your back against the richly packed warm herbal hay. The social and ritual aspects come through an ancient Alpine tradition of maintaining health and well-being.

Hot Tubs

The humble hot tub can serve many roles in the unwinding and socialising of the spa space, from the simple teak Japanese round design with seats, but no jets, to the all singing and dancing fibreglass and moulded designs now available. They can be ridiculously noisy and also quite unattractive, but help people enjoy being in water that gently relaxes their muscles and often serve as pleasurable outside spa-therapy in almost any weather. The trend for de-centralising the spa space means that more hot tubs are being used to fulfil the need to enjoy time relaxing outside in the elements, perhaps sheltered by a gazebo or flexible structure for changing climates. Perfect for full moon nights and white snowy days.

Hydro-pools

These are the evolutionary big brother of the hot tub which harnesses the power of water through a series of creative jets, vibrational pulses and circuits of water that flow imaginatively as mildly therapeutic play areas for pre-treatment relaxation or as a journey within itself. They vary enormously depending on the budget, space and philosophy of the spa and can be integrated into thallasotherapy, hot springs and pure water sources. Normally, hydro-pools will require high levels of chlorine to maintain hygiene, even if ozone systems are employed so they are not recommended to stay in for a long period of time. It is vital to wash before and after using hydro-pools and if possible to steam afterwards to support deep cleansing the skin itself.

Watsu Pools

Watsu has slowly found its way into spas from America where it was created by Harold Dull, a well- known shiatsu practitioner, whilst playing in the water at Harbin Hot Spring in California over 20 years ago. It has grown into a superb all embracing water therapy that requires a water temperature of 37 to 39 degrees in order to be carried out therapeutically. During the watsu treatment where the practitioner supports the client throughout the session within the water, it is vital that the body temperature of approximately 37 degrees is maintained throughout for receptivity, safety and relaxation. This is a meditative and energetic ritual which requires a peaceful and tranquil atmosphere, so a dedicated space is preferable. An optimum size for a one to one watsu pool is about five square metres. However, where a large shared pool temperature is kept at the correct temperature, it is possible to give a watsu as the warm water slows everyone down creating a more meditative environment as maintained in The Bath House at The Royal Crescent in Bath.

Floatation Tanks

Flotation Therapy has become an accepted form of attaining the deep Theta state of relaxation that we discussed in the chapter Your Body which allows right and left sides of the brain to synchronise and generate an altered state of consiousness. A Float Tank contains approximately 12 inches of Epsom salt water solution, maintained at body temperature, upon which you float like the Dead Sea. Within the tank all your senses are subdued by the chamber being completely dark, soundless and still, your body suspended in the water completely free of the pull of gravity. Oxygen and air flow through the tank freely. The sensation is a dissolving of the physical and sensory barriers that usually define us and therefore creates a floating sensation. Almost like being in outer space. This expands the mind and the relationship to the body leading to a state of deep relaxation.

Usually a tank will be situated in a private, secure room where you can control the internal lighting within the tank. Sessions last between 30 minutes to one hour, or longer if you wish, though the salt solution may affect the skin.

Originally called 'Sensory Deprivation Tanks' by John Lilly, the man behind this invention, he created them following his work in the ocean exploring the consciousness of dolphins and the effect of hallucinogenic drugs such as LSD.

Floatation is now used as the ultimate de-stressing therapy that also prove useful environments for listening to subliminal guided relaxation and personal development dialogue, as well as reducing physical discomfort such as lower back pain, migraines, accelerating healing of injuries. Sportsmen and women find floatation a perfect environment for virtual training of techniques and circuits or psychological preparation before a race. Other proven benefits are known to reduce chronic depression, anxiety, insomnia, phobias and high blood pressure.

Dry Floatation Beds

These wonderful multi-purpose water filled dry floatation beds primarily create a weightlessness that totally support the muscular system for maximum relaxation on a physical and psychological level due to the passivity of the experience. As a treatment within itself, whilst listening to guided relaxation or soft music in a low lit space or as an aid to body wraps, the flotation creates a deep sense of receptivity therapeutically calming the nervous system and relieving muscular tensions. Flotation beds can have added features where the water beneath the latex surface is controlled to form soft or powerful movement into specific areas of the body. During a body wrap they provide floatation therapy and on completion can be used to apply a lymphatic drainage massage pulse to shake up and release toxins effortlessly. A great spa therapy aid that clients enjoy as an added bonus to their ritual

Relaxation Spaces

Do not underestimate the importance of peaceful relaxation spaces. They vary enormously according to the philosophy, orientation and location of each spa, whether that is a warm, dimly lit room with comfortable lounging beds, candles, own reading light, aromas, music and refreshments served elegantly, or perhaps a spacious, light, airy environment with vistas and views. A well situated and enjoyable relaxation room is vital for integration of the relaxing benefits of spa-ing and rituals, as well as time for reading, reflection and just being in a beautiful, uplifting, completely stress-free environment. For optimum choice private relaxation spaces are a heavenly luxury that allows those in need of stillness and isolation for deep relaxation, meditation and regenerative sleep to let go into a blissful state without concern of being disturbed; or disturbing others with a snore or two. Ideally, there will be comfortable and varied relaxation areas outside, inside and in privacy as an integral part of the spa facility.

The joy of guiding your client to an inspiring relaxation area after or before a session provides your client with the opportunity to expand their inner journey into peace and well-being.

Therapists Dynamics

Male and Female Therapists Employment

Any spa that you visit shows a predominance of women therapists, particularly in the UK and Europe, whereas in some Indian and American spas there appears to be slightly more of a balance of male therapists. There is also an element of men from those cultures being more involved in holistic massage and beauty therapy, though generally female therapists are more in demand. Where there are traditional ayurvedic treatments an in-depth consultation will often be represented by a male physician and carried out by a male or female practitioner. Certainly there is the fact that most male and female clients would rather be treated by a woman so this will also influence recruitment policies. We know that massage is the number one treatment requested within the spa setting so this is an important skill to cultivate and excel in if you wish to work full-time where so many of the treatments, whether beauty or body are massage based. However, the male therapist who can also offer alongside massage therapy more specific skills, such as sports massage, shiatsu, acupressure or Thai massage, one to one fitness, management skills or life coaching makes them far more employable. A balance of men and women working together creates a healthy flow of yin-yang energy within the overall environment and allows for insight and an added innovation of the services offered.

Client Responses

As hands on body-work is an intimate, sometimes tender and heart-felt experience it can cause your client to have uncontrollable feelings. These feelings may be a sense of vulnerability or emotional and psycho-physiological responses that can arise in a variety of ways such as crying, laughter or sexual arousal. If your client begins to cry uncontrollably, ask them if they would like you to take a break from the treatment, have a glass of water or to continue. Be gentle, compassionate and kind giving your client the space to cry if they need to, though not asking too many questions as you may not be trained to respond appropriately. Kindness and acknowledgement, however, go a long way in supporting them through such a release.

Sexual arousal in men can be totally involuntary and they may well be embarrassed about this, and apologize. In this situation, it is best to be understanding and if the problem continues ask them if they would like a moment to themselves or to discontinue the session. In the event that you begin to feel unsafe or uncomfortable, tell your client that you are a professional therapist and that it would be best to end the session.

When an actual sexual advance in either word or action is made towards you, remove your hands from the client, standing back from the couch, and tell them very clearly the same information suggested above. If this does not work and the client continues to sexually harass you, tell them that this is a professional treatment which cannot be continued in the circumstances. Leave the room and go straight to the management or failing this to a colleague able to support and help you. Following this, management is advised to speak directly with the client and their name is to be listed so that they can be identified as potentially problematic for future reference.

Remember, you are a professional in your area of work and are consequently in charge of the situation in a one to one encounter or therapeutic session with a client. Therefore you are at liberty to refuse to treat this client in the future. In the event that you feel traumatised by such an experience, ask your manager for a counselling session with a recommended counsellor.

Clients Complaints

There is a possibility that a client may make a complaint about you regarding the standard of your treatment, your personal hygiene, or some other dissatisfaction your client has about the session. This could also include a physical problem that arises the next day after a session in the form of muscular pain or strain, skin irritation or the client feeling imbalanced. In these circumstances the consultation form should be checked to see if any contra-indications have not been met by you or whether the client did not answer an important question which could have prevented the problem arising. In relation to skin reactions from products, recommend washing with a mild soap and drinking plenty of water. In these circumstances, sometimes management will think it best to not charge the guest or they may offer another complimentary treatment to make up for the disappointment.

Whatever the case, being understanding and professional with giving helpful information and advice is essential to maintain good relations. Sometimes it can be useful to simply ask the client what they would like the spa to do or offer them, depending, of course, on the integrity of the guest.

If it is more serious and the guest decides to make a case against you, your professional practitioner insurance, or the spas own liability and insurance policy will be able to cover you. When you are employed make sure that your employer is covered by insurance that includes all therapies and therapists working on the premises and under their management. This will not cover any treatments you give anywhere else, so it is always useful and safe to have your own insurance as well.

Accreditation and Insurance

Being employable to carry out professional beauty treatments, spa therapies and massage based treatments requires you to have a recognised qualification and a certain level of experience, often including team work. Professional training qualifications that give you a recognised certificate is essential for being professionally employed and obtaining independent therapists insurance.

Most product houses that provide advanced training in their own specific product knowledge, rituals and treatments will also require that you already have a basic qualification in associated skills which may include aesthetics, anatomy and physiology and first aid. In the UK there are many vocational and advanced training courses in beauty therapy, massage therapy and all the specialised complimentary and holistic therapy skills. Many of these independent training schools and courses will give their own qualification which may or may not be associated with a recognised national or international body. This may or may not be important to you but if you need a recognised certificate make sure that courses you take will give you credits, at least, or the association to a recognised national body.

The main professional standard acknowledged by spa employers, is the National Vocational Qualification (NVQ) which has three levels, and they will require NVQ Level 3 which is the highest level of vocational training units within that system.

There are a number of other recognized Bodies of Authority who serve to accredit courses such as ITEC The International Therapy Examinations Council, who are the largest international examination board offering a variety of qualifications worldwide. In the UK the government accredited Qualification and Curriculum Authority (QCA), on behalf of the Department of Education and Skills is associated with ITEC. Their qualifications are supported by industry and recognised internationally.

The BTEC National Diploma has a system of unit certification bringing people to a basic professional level enabling them for employment in their chosen skills. Assessment is through work assignments on work-related situations or activities that involve study and teamwork.

Other well acknowledged associations are IIHHT International Institute of Health and Holistic Therapies, ICHT International Council of Holistic Therapies, FHT Federation of Holistic Therapists, EdExcel, IFHB International Federation of Health and

Beauty Therapists, PACT Professional Association of Clinical Therapists, HFST International Council of Health, Fitness and Sports Therapists.

However, alongside these there are many other associations that specialise in acknowledging and regulating the professionalism of courses in every area of body therapy, such as shiatsu, deep tissue massage, sports massage, aromatherapy, reiki, reflexology, and natural medicine to name just a few.

Taking all this into account there are a few independent courses and schools in specific therapeutic practices who are not regulated by a national body, yet have a level of excellence in the field that is highly respected by many aware of their training. In this situation a qualification and certificate of completion of training, along with personal recommendation may well be sufficient to employ you, particularly if you are willing to train further.

Working in the USA has very strident law enforcement about practicing massage and all body workers and masseurs require a licence to work professionally. If you are seeking employment in America you may well need to take a course recognised by the National Certification of Practitioners, which has a Code of Honour and a system whereby you accrue credits through courses, or take an examination qualifying and associating you to a school or college whose training is national recognized. You can then apply for a licence.

Insurance
There are now numerous companies whose policies will insure professional and training body and beauty therapists of all disciplines to practice independently. You may have a company recommended to you through the training you have undertaken or through a friend. There are a few recommended here that can be found through the internet and are well-known for their comprehensive and budget sensitive quotes. You may not need your own insurance if you are working under the auspices of a major spa or even urban location, but you must check this out at the time of your employment and make sure it is written into your contract.

This not only protects you, but also your employers who are responsible for their clients' safety and well-being. Keep in mind that if you wish to treat your own private clients outside of your spa employment you will need independent insurance to cover you.

Massage Therapist Liability Insurance
Sinclair Insurance Company Ltd
Namasta
Massage Therapy Insurance
Lloyds Business Insurance

Increasing your chances of employment
As most spa product houses provide specific treatment training, you may be able to take your knowledge and skills from one spa to the next that uses the same brand, or require further training in your new position. However, the best way to increase your chances of employment is to specialise in the more unusual therapeutic skills such as hot stone therapy, reflexology, acupressure, deep tissue massage, shiatsu, watsu and thai yoga massage and ayurvedic therapy, as well as specialised aesthetics like laser hair removal, non-surgical face lifting and light therapy, in addition to your holistic body and or beauty qualification. If you are primarily a body worker with various skills but no direct training in beauty treatments you are still very employable. Your spa may see fit to train you in the more holistic beauty treatments which consist of massage techniques.

In the evolving climate of spas, there is room for more innovation and growth in areas of body mind therapy that supports the fundamental ethos of well-being. Therefore develop skills not many others have and continue to research and train for your future enjoyment and vocational success.

Increasing your chances of employment includes your flexibility as weekends and evenings become optimum times for spas to increase revenue and provide an important service for the working community, so being available at those crucial times is a big plus. Most rotas are fair when everyone can share the later hours and weekends and you may well find greater work opportunities to gain valuable experience when you are just beginning.

Induction and Training Opportunities

Each spa has its own protocols in almost every area of the environment so make sure you receive an adequate induction and orientation training program to help you embrace the philosophy and client care procedures. If such a program does not exist ask for one anyway. You are entitled to have a record of

Your Contract – usually when a trial period has been completed that defines your commitment as an employee and your employers, your salary, holidays, disciplinary procedures and other important company policies and procedures.

Your Job Description – defining your role and skills, spa expectations, management controle, spa mission statement and/or philosophy

Therapy Room Protocols – practicalities of maintaining pristine working conditions

Client Care Protocols – practicalities, communication and procedures of taking care of your clients whilst in the spa and during treatments

Treatment Protocols – training manuals for all treatments you carry out

Product Knowledge – listing of all products key ingredients, contra-indications and best use

Sales Incentives – how to promote products successfully

Performance Bonuses – reaching or exceeding target quota of treatments or sales for rewards

Rotas – an up to date timetable of the whole teams work schedule

Within a busy spa, upgrading standards and further training can often be a challenge to organise due to the ongoing demand on therapists to carry out the daily rota. This is a catch 22 scenario and one which management needs to address as creatively as possible, as the busier the spa, the more need for keeping up to date with training initiatives. Equally, spas who need to improve their service must invest in training their therapists to give them the tools required for success and refinement.

Whenever training is offered, always try to take advantage of it to enhance your overall knowledge and skills. The more you know, the more employable you become enhancing your ability to understand many aspects of the spa culture allowing you to be promoted or considered for a more leading role, if that is what you want.

Creative Product Sales

The requirement on therapists to link treatments to product sales and further bookings can cause inner conflict as some may find it difficult to shift gears from the peace of a healing session to selling a product. The ease of this communication rests in your understanding of how to inspire your client to be interested enough to buy a product as a gradual process. Your client wants to know exactly what they are buying and why they should buy it.

Your role is to softly educate and raise awareness of the therapeutic benefits, during the treatment, by mentioning one or two ingredients in each of the blends that are particularly good for your client. They will be far more open and receptive to what you have to say when they can smell, feel and experience the products in treatment. This does not mean you should over indulge your knowledge by talking throughout the session. Just drop a few seeds of knowledge about some of the therapeutic ingredients that you know will benefit your client when used at home on a regular basis. This also shows your generosity of spirit, to engage your client in the therapeutic process and after treatment care. On conclusion of the session you can suggest they use a particular product at home, reminding them of the ingredient, and ask your spa receptionist to show the client the product package, or do so yourself. Writing down recommendations for products or further treatments on a Spa Prescription Card also provides an ongoing client care philosophy.

Cleanliness is next to Godliness

The spa is a place where people are essentially releasing parts of themselves that are decaying, or dead or has outworn it usefulness, which in Ayurvedic terms are called Malas. A mala is an 'excretion', waste matter, which the body has manufactured and discards through all the avenues and pathways it can find. Ayurveda identifies malas as hair, nails, dried skin, exhalation, perspiration, mucous, urine, waxes, faeces and gas. Through the purifying and detoxifying benefits of spa therapy the body sheds its malas profusely, unplugging and freeing the body and mind for regeneration and healing. The spa can easily become clogged and congested with so much old and dying waste, and therefore should be kept immaculately clean down to the finest detail.

You may well be responsible for cleaning your own treatment room completely on a regular basis and special time needs to be factored into your schedule to do so, if this is the case. In the event that you only *maintain* the hygiene of your work -space, and it is cleaned by a professional cleaner regularly this is by far the best solution. Furniture requires moving, the floor deeply cleansed, all surfaces and areas thoroughly cleaned, perhaps way beyond the level of a personal home or space.

Review your space at the beginning and end of each day and just check what it needs in terms of deep cleaning maintenance and either plan it into your schedule or let management know so cleaners can be adequately instructed.

Conscious Clearing of Your Work Space

Your environment lends itself, like a living creature, to your purpose and aspirations. Your energy can flow more freely through the spaces within and around you when your immediate environment reveals a harmonious organisation that supports your work with a sense of balance and beauty. The spa itself will have specific directives to create a harmonious feeling in the treatment rooms that may well combine, colour with texture, folding of towels, an artistic couch set-up and other objects to enliven and decorate the space. Objects and spaces are forms of energy that *hold* energy, serving as practical tools, yet also have an aesthetic quality to illuminate and transform the dynamics of the workspace.

The process of maintaining the energy in the space combines frequent deep cleaning with daily conscious cleansing of the psychic and emotional energy that can become trapped in the objects, corners and hidden areas of the room. As we discussed the spa is a place where people let go and release the build-up of waste in all its forms, including negative thinking, anxiety, stress, toxicity, anger, sadness or grief.

This 'dross', toxic waste, needs to be cleared from your workspace consciously and with Intention. As you wipe over surfaces and prepare your room for the day or even after a session to begin afresh, feel as though you are clearing away any negative energy and replacing them with the light of your conscious awareness, your love and attention.

Spiritual Room Cleansing
Of great assistance in this process is the burning of certain herbs and roots that have a special significance in purifying an atmosphere. Smoke is an etheric substance that can flow into the vibrational energy fields and diffuse dense areas of formless and invisible waste, generated by psychic or emotional disturbance. Many ancient cultures have used various plants to do exactly this, helping the spirit to move more freely through the space, supporting the complete recycling of unwanted waste energy. Where there is congestion in the space, transformation can be limited and incomplete.

American Indians use `smudge sticks`, a bunch or tightly bound and dried herbs, (which are available from specialist spiritual stores) or you could make them yourself with sage, rosemary, bay and juniper. These sticks are lit then blown out to smoulder, the smoke rising up to permeate the atmosphere. You can also use sprigs of simple dried sage or burn frankincense on a small smouldering charcoal in a bowl of salt. This ritual can also protect you from the possibility of catching any illness and maintains wellbeing.

To cleanse a room carry the stick in your hand and waft it around the room thinking with intent about how you are clearing, purifying and opening up the space. Pay particular attention to the corners of the room circling the smoke into these areas to diffuse and dissolve any blockage to the circulation of fresh energy. To empower this cleansing ritual you may like to sing, chant, say a prayer, or an affirmation of intent.

Objects of Focus
The mind sees unconsciously beyond the physical form, through the obvious periphery of objectivity to the more subtle associations and meaning hidden within the form. Observation creates a relationship to that which you are seeing, creating a response within you, whether you realise it or not. You may ignore things, love things, dislike things, be entertained by things, or simply use those things because they serve as practical tools, yet they nevertheless become a part of your experience.

The purpose of clearing your space allows you to also relate openly with the objects around you so that they support the work processes you undertake. If these objects have been well chosen they will enhance qualities of empathy, creativity, skilfulness and peace for you and your client. Images that inspire, reflecting calming energy are often seen in spas with an eastern influence. Eastern philosophies have a natural feng shui within them and Bhuddas or other symbols that demonstrate tranquillity generally hold the space. If you are responsible for maintaining the tidying of objects in your work space, touch and place them consciously so that they are cared for and appear comfortable in relation to the space. Notice if they appear better with space around them or close to another object. Go on the principle that less is more. If spa protocols allow you may move things from time to time, which can help to re-energise the space, as noticing and paying attention to objects develops an energetic relationship with them. The space becomes your laboratory, where everything within it defines your purpose and goals.

> *And what is it, the heart?*
> *It is the sound of the pine breeze*
> *There in the sumi painting.*

Dainin Katagiri

Crystals in the workspace

The energy and presence you have imbued into this space will support you, even when you are elsewhere. This space is the manifestation of your infra-structure and reflects the respect you have for the life within you; an honouring of the mystery of your being. To sustain this ongoing dynamic crystals and stones can be used to focus and enhance energy and have been used in this way since there has been a history of mankind. Crystals are a unique form of matter that emit a vibration known as the Piesoelectric Effect. This form of subtle electrical energy creates a current that is usable in watches and computers to regenerate their power. This same energy is utilised in crystal healing where the minute movement of minerals within the crystals positively influence our psychological, physical, spiritual and emotional wellbeing. Very sensitive people can feel crystal energy in the form of a heat or pulsation, or simply a deeply relaxed sense of balance.

Within the workspace they offer a wonderful charge to the environment and can be used for their specific individual qualities as well as where you place them. Feng Shui, the oriental art of placement, suggests that you use them above doorways to clear or neutralise the energy moving in and out of the room. If the room has strong beams in the ceiling, hanging crystals from them will lift any oppressive energy that the beam sends down. Using crystals like psycho-spiritual neutralisers is particularly helpful in the therapy room as they diffuse or transform negative forces, breaking them down and directing them to where they originate. Place them in central locations on a surface, or very large ones on the floor.

Cleansing your crystals on a regular basis is essential to maintain their effectiveness. Soak them in pure salts overnight or rub them in heavy salt water, letting them dry naturally. This purifies their power and presence in the work-space.

Crystals can be used within rituals and treatments, to focus, balance and liberate blocked energy. They can now be found in steam rooms and saunas, as key not reception pieces and therapeutic aids in many traditions. Here are some descriptions of useful crystals and stones which have an affinity with your aura, and are therefore very helpful in Chakra Balancing.

Useful Dynamic Crystals

Clear Quartz Crystal

This powerful crystal, known as the grandfather of the mineral kingdom, is utilised for many purposes as it vibrates clear white light which contains all the rays of the rainbow. Quartz is conceived within the womb of the earth, maturing there till excavated, and has the intense ability to dissolve darker karmic tones in the aura. It represents the perfect material to align spiritual energy with physical matter, accelerating individual growth with an integrated awareness and positive energy.

As small hand held crystal wands, or generators, clear quartz makes for an effective tool to focus and channel energy. Small and very large Generator Crystals are faceted on six sides that meet sharply to form a terminated apex.

They are helpful placed above doors, beams, alongside important images, amidst product displays and brochures, next to images of people for healing, magnifying affirmations and prayers. Quartz is exceptionally helpful on or near computers to differ static and negative energy from consuming the user, important on reception desks.

Clusters of single apex crystal formations sharing a common base, living in harmony serves as an excellent room cleanser and a balancing force set between two people generating clarity and balance.

Quartz cultivates positive thought forms through the pineal gland in the crown chakras, opening channels of receptivity, transmitting active energy for purpose and intention. A wonderful crystal to wear whenever you are working on developing more concentration, skill and personal growth.

Make a habit of cleaning the crystal that you wear regularly, and they are best utilised when not worn all the time. Be selective and know why you are wearing it. Knowledge enriches your consciousness.

Amethyst Crystal

The dynamic purple ray of the amethyst crystal is known for its ability to ward off fear and negativity and has been used in many religious and spiritual traditions for this purpose. The pope always wears a large amethyst stone ring to protect him from supposed 'evil' forces. In more spiritual traditions amethyst is used to open the 'third eye', our psychic energy centre at the sixth chakra by clearing away chaotic thought forms for meditation. This enhances intuition and insight. Amethyst vibrates with an intensity that calls for complete letting go and trusting, the amethyst blue ray balancing any red fearful or angry energy from the aura, transforming denser rays to light.

Amethysts affinity with the pituitary gland at the sixth chakra benefits the balance of right and left sides of the brain. Amethyst strengthens the endocrine glands boosting the immune system, cleansing the blood and de-toxifying the body and mind.

Amethysts in large cavernous formations that curve inwards are empowering to catch negativity when placed strategically in an area of stress, whether that is a corner of the room or in a reception area to keep the space light and free. In de-toxifying and de-stressing therapies and rituals this greatly enhances the transformation of negative to positive energy.

As a piece to wear, be careful of its continuous use. Its properties can reduce libido and isolate energy sometimes to the detriment of forming a loving relationship with a partner. However, it is excellent as a protective amulet and therapeutic instrument in treatments.

Rose Quartz Crystal

The soft pink ray of rose quartz sends out a gentle, soothing vibration that has a natural affinity with the heart chakra. Its calming energy can bring qualities of inner peace, healing and sanctuary to our emotions, as well as the psycho-spiritual connection that influence our feelings. The loving vibration of rose can soften the pain of sadness, anxiety, loneliness, bereavement and loss, generating feelings of forgiveness and self-acceptance. Therefore, as an aid for healing Rose Quartz rises as the Mother energy, like a healing balm that can touch the soul. Rose is a slow vibration that is greatly empowered through the conducting energy of healing hands to empower its force, and meditations such as the Metta in Your Spirit also benefit from the kindness of rose quartz.

Rose can however generate emotional release through its softening qualities, and therefore may draw buried emotions to the surface to be released. It is always received well in a therapeutic situation and tumbled rose quartz is ideal to rest on the chest area and as a pendent it falls well on the heart chakra.

Large pieces of rose quartz are not found very often but carvings and sculpture can be found. These exceptional pieces generate a soothing, heart-centred vibration to a space and are wonderful in relaxation areas.

Smokey Quartz Crystal

The all embracing white light of the clear quartz crystal is intensified in this smokey configuration, which serves to ground this light, giving faith and hope to our intentions, prayers and creativity. Smokey helps to manifest our dreams enhancing our potential by dissolving inferior patterns of behaviour that may limit our self-expression. Smokey harnesses our concentration and boosts the endocrine adrenal glands, kidney and pancreas. This is a powerful force of energy to wear occasionally and excellent to use in meditative sessions and areas of the spa.

Amber Stone

Known as 'the mindful one' amber connects us to the past as its source is fossilised resin and therefore holds within it the karma of other living things. It is considered a sacred stone in this respect and was the first known currency in the ice-age. Having a lot of amber was considered a sign of great wealth. Amber can be helpful to draw out the memory and connect us to our own karmic patterns. However, there are those who are suspicious of amber and those who love it, two distinct camps divide the association with this mystical material. Do you have any feelings about it?

Malachite Stone

This enriched mineral stone has an earthy green vibrational colour that is nurturing and regenerative. Pebble stones are usually used in treatments but you can find rough formations that are very powerful as a grounding piece in therapy spaces. It serves to bring the emotions into harmony with the body and is therefore a helpful force for the heart chakra, which we have seen has a pink and green ray of colour. Rose quartz and Green Malachite work well together for an integrated earthy balance.

Citrine Quartz Crystal

The golden ray of citrine connects with the solar plexus at the third chakra and generates qualities of self-esteem and self-confidence by preventing self destructive energies from building up. Benefits boost the function of the liver, spleen, digestive organs, kidneys and colon as well as tissue regeneration. To instil warmth and energy into the body citrine is a good choice. The golden ray brings a sense of abundance and liberation to life. Citrine is usually a rough edged crystal yet has cheerful and happy vibrational qualities for healing.

Bloodstone

Blood stone is a variety of chalcedony that is excellent for circulation, improving the oxygenation of the blood stream enhancing physical and mental vitality. The benefits influence the heart, spleen and enrich bone marrow so is excellent for arthritic, rheumatic problems, cold hands and feet, as well as the aging process. Bloodstone reduces physical tensions in the muscles and joints reducing overall stress.

Turquoise Stone

Turquoise is known for its ability to ward off the negative effects of radiation and environmental pollution. It protects and strengthens skin from the inside out and deepens the absorption of nutrients. Turquoise enhances friendships and communication with its affinity with the throat chakra that has a vibrational blue ray, cultivating strong bonds and loyalty.

As a powerful aid to those working long hours in the city, or in an artificial environment, a turquoise stone on the desk and by a phone is a great asset to the workplace. Wearing turquoise is also an attractive force opening up the channels for new friendships and sharing empathetically.

As a healing aid for those going through chemotherapy or other forms of invasive surgery this is a useful tool.

Tigers Eye Stone

This mysteriously attractive stone that transforms in different lights is connected to the root chakra, your sense of groundedness and survival instincts. The benefits contribute towards overcoming anguish or petty jealousies and brings qualities of physical self awareness and balance. Excellent for those who need a little bravery to make a change in their lives and also stimulates the break down of food through the digestive system, improving elimination. The pebble stones can be placed on the root chakra at the base of the spine or lower abdomen, or wear it to gain insight into the direction you need to go in your life when change is on the table.

Tourmaline

Tourmalines come in many colours, the green ray particularly being of great benefit. The green healing vibration of the crystal enhances qualities of sensitivity and the way through difficulties and psychological imbalance. Known to help mental disorders by strengthening the inner centre and connection with others. Use green tourmaline when life seems to have got out of hand and you are spending too much time analysing and behaving irrationally. This will put you in touch with your core strength and heart chakra. In the same way you can use this in treatments to help balance your clients if there is an excess of nervous energy.

Moonstones

The changing colours and rays of light that moonstones transmit, harmonise well with female energy and are known for their association with fertility and rebalancing hormonal and menstrual imbalance. Therefore it has a strong association with emotional wellbeing and is sometimes thought of as The Mother Earth of stones. The nurturing wisdom within the vibrational field has an affinity with the second chakra where our resources of creative energy are generated and stored. The connection with the moon makes them a reflective stone that also enhances intuition and psychic awareness. Wear and use wisely.

Flourite Stone

Flourite too comes in many colours and is known as The Gatherer as its strong qualities help the body absorb vital nutrients that strengthen teeth, bones, and improve blood circulation. The qualities are useful where there is degeneration or weakness within the skeletal system and brings patience to those who are irritable and implusive.

Lapiz Lazuli Stone

Lapiz corrals extraoradinary minerals within that give it a rich vibrant energy. Flecked with gold and of a true azure type blue its softness and flexibility makes it perfect jewellery, especially as a necklace. The blue ray harmonises the fifth chakra at the throat encouraging clear communication and speech. The ancient Egyptians prized lapis as a symbol of spiritual wealth and liberation, carving sacred symbols and forms out of it, as well as wearing it profusely. Its magical energy is a strong friend if you are teaching or guiding others, and also helps to heal any blockages from the throat chakra which connects up with our sense of 'hearing,' so necessary in today's world.

Sound Pollution

The operational sounds within the environment, is a consideration that needs to be factored into the overall design right at the start of a new project. This will include where the pool plant is located, how other machine driven equipment might affect the general ambience and the proximity of doors, showers and changing rooms to relaxation spaces. There needs to be clear definition between busy areas and quiet space so if these structural design features are not well thought through a sense of harmony can elude the place.

As a therapist you can do your best to move with awareness through all areas especially around treatment rooms and where people are relaxing. Wearing soft shoes reduces noise and you can also take special care to walk toe to heel to minimise vibrations through the floor when walking fast past closed doors. Closing doors softly and carefully will also reduce sound pollution, making sure that any creaky hinges are oiled and closure is smooth. Felt cushioning for reducing banging of doors are helpful aids. If you are aware of a persistent noise in your room that you know should not be there, report it to your manager or straight to maintenance.

Music and natural sound recordings have become synonymous with well-being and the choice of music and volume level it is played is to be seriously considered. Music needs to have quality so that it does not become wall to wall carpeting for the ears, but actually adds another dimension to the treatment and other areas, yet not too loudly as it can dominate and interfere with the subtle aspects of rituals. If music is piped through to all rooms from a central source make sure whatever is chosen is changed frequently. The choices are vast today and the best route to go is a combination of instrumental western, eastern or ethnic composition that has harmony and inspiration without being synthesized. Birdsong and water, bells and chanting can be meditative sounds for relaxation and meditation areas.

Pure Hearing

Hearing, like breathing, happens all by itself. Whether you choose to hear the everyday sounds around you or not, you will be aware of them on one level or another. Even familiar sounds can dynamically influence the way we feel. Like aromas, sounds carry an association which trigger emotional and psycho-physiological responses. Sounds can generate blocked, tense or resistant feelings, whereas others may be soothing and inspirational. Sounds can and do transmit a quality, a vibration that can physically soften or tighten muscles and joints, influencing our thought processes and state of mind.

Hearing is a vital part of living, and though equal in importance to all our other senses, deafness does not mean you cannot `tune in` to vibrations and qualities of sound just as Mozart did when he cut the legs off his piano and placed his ear to the floor, to receive the notes vibrations. Sounds *are* vibrations of energy that resonates through us at varying intensities, creating patterns of sensations to which we intuitively respond.

Your own voice reveals unique qualities about you which can be recognized like your signature or how you walk. Other peoples` voices may attract or repel you, communicating a living energy that influences our relationship to that person. The tone and energy within the voice is directly linked to the way we breathe and consequently to the rhythm of our thinking and emotional content. A peaceful person will naturally pace their breath with more awareness, allowing more prana to circulate through their language and thought processes. Stillness and pause, will punctuate their speech so that the vibration and energy transmitted is harmonious. By learning how to listen, how to hear with your whole being, body, mind and soul, you will begin to attune yourself to a more subtle resonance influencing the sound of your own voice.

For example, a vital element of practicing yoga with a teacher is that you can **allow** the sound of the teachers' voice **in,** to guide you. The voice itself is an instruction which can dissolve layers of tension simply by hearing their tone. The voice is a thread that inspires you to focus your mind and work with any tensions you may be experiencing so that they can be transformed. Qualities of trust and empathy, of understanding and compassion are expressed through a guiding voice.

Often our ability to listen is limited by what we *anticipate* hearing, or expect to hear. We are conditioned to listen for certain sounds and respond out of sheer habit. As many of the sounds around us are inauthentic, harsh or unpleasantly repetitious we may block or create barriers of tension around our inner ear which develops an unconscious relationship to the sound affecting our level of relaxed awareness. Superficially this ability to ignore sounds can be temporarily helpful, but over the long-term irritations build up and are released through nervous energy, anger, or even tinnitus, an insistent buzzing in the inner ear. In this context, it is **how** we **relate to** sound that opens the pathway to relaxation, balance and inner peace. The sounds within the spa need to awaken this inner ear, through water, well chosen music, birdsong, bells and the therapists caring attuned voice.

All the meditations and practices in this handbook will help you to connect with your own sound, and create healing, harmonious qualities. Primarily you need to know how to listen, how to hear with your whole attention, your whole being.

Hearing without resistance or judgement will create a receptivity in your mind that influences your physical well-being. Noise pollution is part of modern technology for which we need to find a balance. It is your awareness that changes how sounds will affect you. When you know how even unpleasant noises can become tools for meditation and relaxation you will experience a wonderful sense of expansive relaxation. If you assume what your response will be, you may well be setting yourself up creating unnecessary negativity such as anxiety or nervous tension. Letting go of expectation relaxes the inner ear allowing sounds to freely travel through you. You will rise above any resistance and take refuge in your inner receptivity giving you a still, strong centre.

By practising this hearing meditation you will become more sensitive to the inner sound of your own voice and therefore be able to express yourself more harmoniously. This is deeply relaxing and therapeutic for you and your client. This meditation is a way in which you can enlighten your mind and heart through hearing.

Hearing Meditation

Find a comfortable place to sit alone, perhaps near sounds of nature or simply indoors.

You can practice this meditation anywhere at all and when your hearing becomes more sensitive you can leave your eyes open. Practice on a crowded tube at rush hour, in a waiting room for an appointment, or when you are working peacefully giving a treatment.

Close your eyes and be as still as possible
Begin by simply being aware of your breathing

Imagine that your ears are like antennae
That they fill the space around you
Let your hearing be your most important sense
Focus entirely on sound

Breathe slowly and deeply
Listening attentively to the sounds around you
letting them pass through you

Notice any resistance or tension to certain sounds
Any attractions or repulsions
Breath into those feelings
Allowing all those sounds to flow through you
Let go of identifying or labelling sounds

`traffic` `bird` `fridge` etc: and
just allow yourself to receive the sounds without
any interpretation
Just let your hearing happen

Listen from the beginning of a sound
through the whole duration
to the fading away of it

Simply allow the sounds to run their course
without analysis or rejection.
And without holding on to them
Open to the sounds around you,
Let them flow through you
Become absorbed into hearing,
Breathing peacefully
Receptive, open and relaxed.

ॐ

The softest thing in the universe
Overcomes the hardest thing in the universe.
That without substance can enter where there is no room.
Teaching without words and work without doing
Are understood by very few.

Lao Tsu ' Tao Te Ching'
Translation by Gia-Fu Feng

Tara Jacqualine Herron has travelled extensively since 1978 living and working in remote and state of the art spas and retreats worldwide. Living in America and Hawaii for ten years, practicing meditation and healing at the Zen Diamond Sangha, Maui, and Vipassana in Massachusetts. Having trained with eminent teachers such as Aitkin Roshi in Hawaii, Dr Vasant Ladd in Sante Fe New Mexico in Ayurveda, The Insight Meditation Society in Massachusetts, Dr George Dodd in Aromatics; Phil Caylor in Deep Tissue Massage and Polarity Therapy at Harbin Hot Springs, Psychic Healing at the Berkley Psychic Institute; Yoga Therapy at the Shivananda Yoga Centre SF, and Kundalini Yoga with Mursid Isa Kadre, amongst many others.

For the past twenty years she has taught yoga and integrative body work, offering one to one sessions, courses and retreats. Her school **Evolve** which is now a spa consultancy, taught diploma courses in aromatherapy and managing stress for ten years, and now develops own brand therapeutic spa products, and treatment rituals. **Evolve** works in collaboration withon new spa projects, creating signature therapeutic treatments and products with professional training programs. Tara offers a coaching service utilising all her skills, maintaining a meditative approach throughout her work. She is available internationally to give workshops, talks, retreats and training of Spa Therapists body, Mind and Soul.

Taras' CDs on some of the meditations and relaxations in this handbook are available by email, please see her web site below

www.yogicsolutions.com